THE TURBULENT 60s

1963

William S. McConnell, *Book Editor*

DISCARD

Bonnie Szumski, *Publisher*
Scott Barbour, *Managing Editor*
David M. Haugen, *Series Editor*

GREENHAVEN
PRESS ®

THOMSON

GALE

San Diego • Detroit • New York • San Francisco • Cleveland
New Haven, Conn. • Waterville, Maine • London • Munich

© 2004 by Greenhaven Press. Greenhaven Press is an imprint of The Gale Group, Inc., a division of Thomson Learning, Inc.

Greenhaven® and Thomson Learning™ are trademarks used herein under license.

For more information, contact
Greenhaven Press
27500 Drake Rd.
Farmington Hills, MI 48331-3535
Or you can visit our Internet site at http://www.gale.com

Cover credit: © Flip Schulke/CORBIS
Library of Congress, 67, 93, 103
National Archives, 10, 15, 114

LIBRARY OF CONGRESS CATALOGING-IN-PUBLICATION DATA

1963 / William S. McConnell, book editor.
   p. cm. — (The turbulent 60s)
Includes bibliographical references and index.
ISBN 0-7377-1502-2 (alk. paper) — ISBN 0-7377-1503-0 (pbk. : alk. paper)
   1. United States—History—1961–1969—Sources. 2. Nineteen sixty-three, A.D.—Sources. I. McConnell, William S. II. Series.
E841.A154 2004
973.922—dc22   2003054322

Printed in the United States of America

CONTENTS

FOREWORD

The 1960s were a period of immense change in America. What many view as the complacency of the 1950s gave way to increased radicalism in the 1960s. The newfound activism of America's youth turned an entire generation against the social conventions of their parents. The rebellious spirit that marked young adulthood was no longer a stigma of the outcast but rather a badge of honor among those who wanted to remake the world. And in the 1960s, there was much to rebel against in America. The nation's involvement in Vietnam was one of the catalysts that helped galvanize young people in the early 1960s. Another factor was the day-to-day Cold War paranoia that seemed to be the unwelcome legacy of the last generation. And for black Americans in particular, there was the inertia of the civil rights movement that, despite seminal victories in the 1950s, had not effectively countered the racism still plaguing the country. All of these concerns prompted the young to speak out, to decry the state of the nation that would be their inheritance.

The 1960s, then, may best be remembered for its spirit of confrontation. The student movement questioned American imperialism, militant civil rights activists confronted their elders over the slow progress of change, and the flower children faced the nation's capitalistic greed and conservative ethics and opted to create a counterculture. There was a sense of immediacy to all this activism, and people put their bodies on the line to bring about change. Although there were reactionaries and conservative holdouts, the general feeling was that a united spirit of resistance could stop the inevitability of history. People could shape their own destinies, and together they could make a better world. As sixties chronicler Todd Gitlin writes, "In the Sixties it seemed especially true that History with a capital H had come down to earth, either interfering with life or making it possible: and that within History, or threaded through it, people were living with a supercharged density: lives were bound up with one another, making claims on one another, drawing one another into the common project."

Perhaps not everyone experienced what Gitlin describes, but few would argue that the nation as a whole was left untouched by the radical notions of the times. The women's movement, the civil rights movement, and the antiwar movement left indelible marks. Even the hippie movement left behind a relaxed morality and a more ecological mindset. Popular culture, in turn, reflected these changes: Music became more diverse and experimental, movies adopted more adult themes, and fashion attempted to replicate the spirit of uninhibited youth. It seemed that every facet of American culture was affected by the pervasiveness of revolution in the 1960s, and despite the diversity of rebellions, there remained a sense that all were related to, as Gitlin puts it, "the common project."

Of course, this communal zeitgeist of the 1960s is best attributed to the decade in retrospect. The 1960s were not a singular phenomenon but a progress of individual days, of individual years. Greenhaven Press follows this rubric in The Turbulent Sixties series. Each volume of this series is devoted to the major events that define a specific year of the decade. The events are discussed in carefully chosen articles. Some of these articles are written by historians who have the benefit of hindsight, but most are contemporary accounts that reveal the complexity, confusion, excitement, and turbulence of the times. Each article is prefaced by an introduction that places the event in its historical context. Every anthology is also introduced by an essay that gives shape to the entire year. In addition, the volumes in the series contain time lines, each of which gives an at-a-glance structure to the major events of the topic year. A bibliography of helpful sources is also provided in each anthology to offer avenues for further study. With these tools, readers will better understand the developments in the political arena, the civil rights movement, the counterculture, and other facets of American society in each year. And by following the trends and events that define the individual years, readers will appreciate the revolutionary currents of this tumultuous decade—the turbulent sixties.

The Year of Confrontation

T he summer of 1963 was the beginning of an end to white racial superiority in the United States. Student and black activists were gaining national media attention through a series of well-planned protests designed to end segregation in public schools, universities, and other public facilities. Government officials developed pending legislation that could end the practice of Jim Crow legislation in the South and ensure equal access to civil liberties on a national level. Marches against local bans on public demonstrations challenged civic authority and paved the way for the "March on Washington" in August, an action that would stand as a lasting symbol of black and white unity against the cause of segregationists.

Although the summer of 1963 showed great promise in changing the lives of black Americans for both present and future generations, the same summer was marked by high-profile events that showed a determined resistance to change. Police chief Joseph "Bull" Connor of Birmingham, Alabama, unleashed dogs and used fire hoses against blacks who marched in downtown Birmingham to protest segregation. Governor George Wallace of Alabama made his final stand against segregation by blocking the entrance of the University of Alabama in an attempt to prevent the registration of two black students. Mississippi senator James O. Eastland held up President John F. Kennedy's new civil rights legislation in a filibuster in the U.S. Senate. Finally, some individuals who did not have the authority of a public office took action against civil rights activists in an attempt to block changes in the South. Many of those resistance efforts were covert and bloody. Prominent civil rights activist Medgar Evers was killed in his driveway in Jackson, Mississippi, and in

September, four young black girls were killed in a church bomb-ing in Birmingham.

The violence was initiated not only against civil rights work-ers and innocent children, but also against government officials who supported civil rights legislation. On November 22, 1963, President Kennedy collapsed under an assassin's bullet while rid-ing in a motorcade through downtown Dallas. This event marked the year as one of disillusionment as well as rage, for the presi-dent's death not only crushed the hopes of African Americans, but left many of the ideals of white America in a sudden state of uncertainty. The year 1963 may well have initiated a new direc-tion of positive change for black Americans, but the cost of such change left a shadow on the remains of the naive idealism that had carried over from the Eisenhower era, a shadow that would haunt the United States throughout the rest of the decade.

The First Stages of Discontent

Ever since the successes of the 1950s, African Americans in 1963 were not content with sitting idly by, waiting for a passive federal government to free them from the new slavery of Jim Crow legis-lation. In 1954, public schools were desegregated by the Supreme Court decision *Brown v. Board of Education.* In 1955, Martin Luther King Jr. desegregated the public transportation system of Montgomery, Alabama, by leading the Montgomery bus boycott. In 1962, King and his associate, Ralph D. Abernathy, another prominent civil rights activist, were arrested in Albany, Georgia, spurring the Albany movement, which helped break down dis-crimination against blacks in that community. And in 1963, due to lack of integration in public schools, the U.S. Supreme Court redefined the concept of "deliberate speed," established in the *Brown v. Board of Education* decision, which defined the pace at which barriers to equality in public schools were to be broken. The court stated, "It was never contemplated that the concept of 'de-liberate speed' would countenance indefinite delay in eliminating racial barriers in public schools. . . . The basic guarantees of our Constitution are warrants for the here and now, and unless there is an overwhelmingly compelling reason, they are to be promptly fulfilled."[1]

The Kennedy administration was also slow to act on the is-sue of civil rights. Although President Kennedy and his brother, Attorney General Robert Kennedy, were friendly to King and other activists, they did little legislatively to enact any change and only acted when it seemed imperative to do so. *Time* magazine reported in June 1963 that President Kennedy's hesitation on civil rights was due to a loss of political support for his "New Frontiers" legislation, which was designed to carry the United States into space as well as build broad social programs for the poor. Kennedy did not want to offend southern Democrats who supported segregation, and therefore he was hesitant to develop civil rights legislation until after the passage of his platform programs. *Time* reported that "Jack and Bobby Kennedy both genuinely believed in equal rights. But as it happens, there is such a thing as practical politics—and the Kennedys figured that they would need Southern Democratic votes in Congress if the New Frontier's legislative programs were to have a chance of passage."[2]

Due to the president's hesitation, several prominent African Americans expressed rage and discontent at the slow pace at which the federal government moved on the issue of civil rights. Author James Baldwin, singers Lena Horn and Harry Belafonte, playwright Lorraine Hansberry, and psychologist Kenneth Clark

John F. Kennedy greets voters during his 1961 presidential campaign. His assassination in 1963 shocked the nation.

participated in a closed-door meeting with Robert Kennedy. According to *Time* magazine, "Bobby went into the meeting under the illusion that Negroes feel gratitude toward the [Kennedy] administration. What he encountered was a shouting, finger-shaking barrage of anger, disappointment, and impatience." Baldwin commented that "Bobby Kennedy was a little surprised at the depth of Negro feeling. We were a little shocked at the depth of his naïveté."[3]

The report card on the Kennedy administration's civil rights position was dissatisfactory. Public opinion about President Kennedy's inaction actually forced a shift in his civil rights strategy. In early June, the president sent a package of civil rights legislation to Congress. The package included measures to fortify voting rights; ban discrimination in hotels, motels, and restaurants; and give the attorney general broader powers to intervene in school segregation cases. The legislation, although highly anticipated by civil rights leaders and many northern Democrats, would face a long delay in passage. After finally passing through the House of Representatives on February 26, 1964, it was tied up in the Senate by a Republican-sponsored filibuster, which did not end until July 1964.

Bull Connor's Use of Dogs and Hoses

In Birmingham, Alabama, police chief Joseph "Bull" Connor was a hard-line segregationist. He had little tolerance for individuals seeking to end discrimination, and he did little to investigate the violence and intimidation against many activists who conducted their work in his city. Segregation was still the law of the land as far as the citizens of Birmingham were concerned, despite Supreme Court decisions to the contrary. According to biographer William A. Nunnelly, Connor, upon winning the post of commissioner of public safety in 1957, stated, "These laws [of segregation] are still constitutional and I promise you that until they are removed from the ordinance books of Birmingham and the statute books of Alabama, they will be enforced in Birmingham to the utmost of my ability and by all lawful means."[4]

In May 1963, tensions between police and activists were at an unmanageably high level. Bull Connor, seeking to keep the status quo, advised his police officers to confront activists as they marched through downtown Birmingham. The protesters were mostly black and included women and children. The police were arrayed in riot gear, including helmets, shields, and batons. The police also had dogs on leashes. Chief Connor had his officers unleash the dogs and set them upon the demonstrators. He also ordered firefighters to use their hoses on the protesters, shooting streams of water at one hundred pounds per square inch. This dangerous, almost deadly use of force garnered the attention of the federal government and gave the idling civil rights movement some much-needed stimulation. As Nunnelly observes in his biography of Connor, "The confrontation between grim-faced, helmeted policemen and their dogs, and black children chanting freedom songs and hymns . . . moved President John F. Kennedy to remark that 'The civil rights movement should thank God for Bull Connor. He's helped it as much as Abraham Lincoln.'"[5] President Kennedy's sentiment is echoed by attorney and book critic Jolanta Juszkiewicz, who notes that "Bull Connor, a man of humble roots and limited ambitions, was determined to perpetuate the status quo even if that meant resorting to strong-arm tactics."[6] This example of violence used by civic authorities in Birmingham illustrated the dire necessity for the federal government to assist African Americans in their struggle for equality. It also brought the cruel oppression of Jim Crow into the homes of white families across the nation via televised reports of the police violence. This turned public sentiment against the South, bringing much needed white sympathy and activism to the civil rights movement.

The Sound of a Rifle, the Rage of a Riot

Black activism, however, was still at the forefront of change. In the South, black activists were hopeful but cognizant of the power that whites held. Medgar Evers once stated about Mississippi, "It may sound funny, but I love the South. I don't choose to live anywhere else. There's land here, where a man can raise cattle, and I'm going to do it some day. There are lakes where a man can sink a hook and fight the bass. There is room here for my children to play and grow, and become good citizens—if the white man will let them."[7] Evers was a young, intelligent, idealistic black man who saw segregation as an obstacle that needed to be dealt with through direct confrontation. Evers was known for speaking his mind regarding his dislike of the inequality that southern Blacks faced every day, and he viewed Mississippi as his battleground. His love for that land exceeded his hate for the institution of segregation. When he was appointed to the position of Mississippi national field secretary for the National Association for the Advancement of Colored People (NAACP) in 1954, Evers finally had a political vantage point from which he could make his case against segregation.

Evers worked hard, sacrificing the financial comforts that a better-paying job would have afforded his family. In an interview for the *Negro History Bulletin*, Evers's wife, Myrlie Evers, stated, "He had no interest in money, fame or any of the other trappings of power and influence. I used to tell him . . . to keep fighting but also to do something for his family as well. He would always say, 'No, my fight is here [and] I don't care if I'm poor.'"[8] In his position as field secretary, Evers diligently worked to register voters, integrate public schools, and end discrimination in public facilities. And although he remained poor, he worked for what he viewed as a higher cause, because he believed in making life better for African Americans in Mississippi.

Evers naturally had enemies. No one can challenge a political system as inherently ingrained in southern society and culture as segregation and not develop political enemies. In 1962, with the successful attempt by James Meredith to integrate the University of Mississippi, Evers stepped up his own political campaign in Jackson by conducting more frequent voter registration drives. Evers worked door to door, oftentimes with little help, motivating blacks in Jackson to join the NAACP to help protest against the Jim Crow laws. His actions were overt and in direct conflict with the beliefs of local residents and public officials. One local resident and member of the Ku Klux Klan, Byron De La Beckwith, planned the murder of Medgar Evers. He created a crawl space in the bushes across the street from the Evers home. On June 12, 1963, Beckwith lay in the bushes with a rifle, waiting for Evers to arrive home from work. When Evers pulled into his driveway and got out of his car, Beckwith shot Evers in the back. Beckwith was eventually arrested for the murder, but he was found not guilty by an all-white jury in 1964. Thirty years later, Mississippi attorney Bobby Delaughter undertook the challenge of bringing Beckwith to justice. Beckwith was finally convicted of Medgar Evers's murder in 1994. The national director of the Anti-Defamation League, Abraham H. Fox, stated after the conviction, "This verdict serves justice in a pivotal case of the civil rights era: the assassination of the Mississippi head of the NAACP amidst the most violent and concerted effort to resist desegregation in American history. The conviction sends a clear signal that racial hatred will not go unpunished in this country."[9]

Following Evers's murder, hundreds of blacks rioted in the streets of Jackson. Police corralled the rioters at the local fairgrounds, where they were kept for several days. During this time, the crowds never stopped yelling and protesting the murder. Jackson city council member Doris P. Smith remembers the action: "We spent three or four days on those fairgrounds under unbearable conditions. We figured the only way out was to aggravate them to death, so we yelled our way out of jail."[10] When the protesters were finally released, local authorities had no choice but to review the policy of segregation and begin instituting changes to the ordinance books. Today, Evers's work has been realized through the opportunities that abound for southern blacks. Jackson, Mississippi, now leads the nation in having the highest number of black officials holding public office. Evers's work to gain the vote has indeed paid off for Mississippi blacks and for blacks in the entire South.

Marching on Washington, D.C.

Two months after Evers's murder, southern blacks brought protest out of the South to the doorsteps of the nation's capital. The March on Washington, on August 28, 1963, was orchestrated by the famous labor leader A. Philip Randolph. He had originally planned such a march for the summer of 1941 as a way to guarantee equal pay and working conditions for blacks, but the effort was postponed due to labor agreements reached with Franklin D. Roosevelt, the president at the time. By 1963, urgent action was needed in order to confront the intolerable degree of inequality that still beleaguered the lives of all blacks in America. Randolph worked closely with several civil rights groups and leaders, including the NAACP, Martin Luther King, and the Student Nonviolent Coordinating Committee (SNCC), to turn his old labor march into a much broader protest. The various groups and individuals worked diligently throughout the summer of 1963, organizing buses, trains, and workers to coordinate such a large-scale event. The march attracted more than 250,000 participants and still stands as one of the largest civil rights protest actions in history. The people flooded into the nation's capital from all over the country, but especially from the Deep South.

Many officials feared that violence was sure to erupt at such a

On August 28, 1963, more than 250,000 people participated in the
March on Washington, one of the largest civil rights protests in history.

gathering. Fortunately, Roy Wilkins of the NAACP met with local police authorities and coordinated a strategy that would not
threaten the crowds and incite them to riot. This included banning
the use of mounted police, who would seem threatening, as well
as keeping riot police well-removed from the route of the march.
The route ended at the base of the Lincoln Memorial. People
stood shoulder to shoulder, remaining quiet so they could hear the
voices of the speakers. Finally, after several hours of speakers, including SNCC speaker Stokely Carmichael, Martin Luther King
gave his historic "I Have a Dream" speech. According to civil
rights activist and former president of the National Council of Negro Women, Dr. Dorothy I. Height, "His message pointed out the
country's glaring shortcomings, yet he never sounded a negative
note. He spoke with a vision of the beloved community. His commitment to love and peace through justice was evident."[11] The
March on Washington had the potential to become a tragedy of
violent confrontation between thousands of police officers and a
quarter of a million people, but well-planned strategies and coordinated efforts made it instead a lasting symbol of the power of
peaceful protest. In the wake of the violence of 1963, this march

was welcomed by activists and politicians alike as a stimulus toward ending the civil rights dispute without further bloodshed.

The Expensive Price Tag of Freedom

Throughout the months preceding the March on Washington, as well as in the weeks following it, southern blacks who tried to register to vote, and those who supported them, continued to be harassed, beaten, and killed. Several instances of violence filled local newspapers across the South. Mississippi and Alabama were two of the most violent states when it came to confronting civil rights activities. In 1963, following the death of Medgar Evers, Reverend George Lee of Belzoni, Mississippi, was murdered when he refused to remove his name from a list of registered voters. Then, local farmer Herbert Lee of Liberty, Mississippi, was killed for having participated in voter education classes. Three other activists who had come to Mississippi to organize voter registration drives—Michael Schwerner, James Chaney, and Andrew Goodman—disappeared in June 1964. Their bodies were discovered several months later outside Philadelphia, Mississippi.

Violence was also aimed at those who worked to desegregate interstate transit systems. These black and white workers were called Freedom Riders because they traveled from northern cities by bus, car, and train to reach the South. In Anniston, Alabama, one bus was firebombed, forcing its passengers to flee for their lives. In Birmingham, black students who rode the buses were severely beaten. In Montgomery, a mob attacked another busload of riders. If arrested, the Freedom Riders did not fare much better in the hands of police. Freedom Riders were lodged in small jail cells and were chosen randomly to be beaten. In the streets, the Freedom Riders joined mass demonstrations where the violent response of local police shocked the naive television audience of America, making not only national headlines but world headlines as well. In Birmingham, police continued the practice of unleashing dogs into peaceful crowds of demonstrators. But the more violent these southern whites became, the more their actions were publicized and denounced across the nation.

The Sixteenth Street Baptist Church Bombing

While Freedom Riders desegrated transit lines and registered voters, King and other civil rights activists were gaining ground in other arenas. By continuing to protest policies that supported inequality, black activists filled jails, clogged city streets, and brought white businesses close to financial ruin for continuing to disallow blacks the same treatment as their white counterparts. Although the success of nonviolent demonstrations provided hope to the movement, it also invited violence. Most protesters accepted that participation in a civil rights demonstration in 1963 invited a hostile response—whether by fire hose, police dog, or police baton. Innocent bystanders, however, made no such decision. Since the South was in a state of turmoil, no one expected that the innocent would always be spared. What was unexpected was the extent of violence directed against innocent lives by the increased fervor of the segregationists.

On Sunday morning, September 15, 1963, the Ku Klux Klan bombed the Sixteenth Street Baptist Church in Birmingham, Alabama, killing four girls. The church had served as the center of life for Birmingham's African American community since its construction in 1911. The four girls killed—Addie Mae Collins, Denise McNair, Carole Robertson, and Cynthia Wesley—were in the basement of the church getting ready for the morning's church service.

Four men were accused of the bombing. They were Thomas Blanton, Robert Chambliss, Herman Cash, and Bobby Frank Cherry. Thomas Blanton was finally convicted of the bombing in 2001 and sentenced to life in prison. Robert Chambliss was tried in 1977 and has since died in prison. Herman Cash died before going to trial. Bobby Frank Cherry was to be tried with Blanton in 2001, but he was found unfit to stand trial because he suffered from dementia.

After the bombing, King came to Birmingham to give the eulogy for the four girls. Also at the funeral was King's friend Fred Shuttlesworth, who remarks that King's eulogy "portrays these four innocents as entering life only briefly, playing nobly and well their parts on the stage of history, and then moving through the curtain back into eternity." King's words revealed the enormity of the crime against innocent lives, compelling white America to reevaluate its policy of denying equality to citizens of the world's greatest nation. Shuttlesworth reinforces this questioning of the American value system by stating that the eulogy is aimed at "those who should be active and vocal in the crusade for freedom and dignity: the silent minister, the vacillating politician, the compromising federal government, and the Negro who accepts segregation without comment."[12] Dr. King's call to conscience promoted a continued commitment to nonviolence and urged the federal government to make a definitive stand against segregation so that the sacrifice of these four children would not be in vain.

The End of Innocence

The assassination of President Kennedy on November 22, 1963, marked the end of innocence for many Americans. *New York Times* Washington correspondent Tom Wicker notes that, at the end of that day, after filing his coverage of the assassination with the news desk, "It was then that I remembered John F. Kennedy's obituary . . . it was still lying on my desk in Washington, not updated, not rewritten, a monument to the incredibility of that afternoon in Dallas."[13] It was Wicker's job to cover the news from Washington, and part of that job was to keep up-to-date records on the president. His sentiment regarding an unfinished obituary seemed to echo what every American thought when Lee Harvey Oswald killed the president: that the age of innocence was over, that America was truly heading into times of uncertainty.

Although President Kennedy was not an agitator for civil rights, his administration was sympathetic to the goals of civil rights activists. His death meant the loss of a valuable ally in an unfinished chapter in American history. The hopes of civil rights leaders now rested on the shoulders of an untried president, Lyndon B. Johnson. Johnson's political views were aligned with Kennedy's, but shaped by a federal government and military leadership that were pushing America away from domestic issues in order to prepare for full-scale involvement in the tiny country of Vietnam.

The year 1963 hailed many landmark achievements in the effort to improve life for a largely unrepresented section of American society. Civil rights leaders would see the fruits of their labor in the passage of the Civil Rights Act in July 1964. America would finally make good on its promise to include blacks in the American dream by making it illegal for state governments to discriminate against any of their citizens.

The violence that characterized 1963 did not end with the death of a president. The surge of power that many people felt in 1963 was later applied to other civil rights protests in the mid-sixties.

As the Vietnam era began and America began shipping many poor, rural blacks across the globe to fight a war against communism, many social activists found it necessary to forgo nonviolent resistance and replace it with direct confrontation, including violence as a means to an end. The year 1963 set the stage for many political victories, but the rage and violent confrontation of the year marred much of the decade that was still to come.

Notes

1. Lucas A. Powe Jr., *The Warren Court and American Politics.* Cambridge, MA: Harvard University Press, 2000.

2. *Time*, "The Nation," June 21, 1963, p. 15.

3. *Time*, "The Negroes Push for Equality," May 17, 1963, p. 27.

4. William A. Nunnelly, *Bull Connor.* Tuscaloosa: University of Alabama Press, 1991, p. 61.

5. Nunnelly, *Bull Connor*, p. 163.

6. Jolanta Juszkiewicz, "Book Review: *Bull Connor*," *Law and Politics Book Review*, January 1992, p. 1.

7. Medgar Evers, "Why I Live in Mississippi," *Ebony*, November 1958, p. 69.

8. Jeffrey Elliot, "Medgar Evers: A Personal Portrait," *Negro History Bulletin*, November/December 1977, p. 760.

9. Anti-Defamation League, "Beckwith Conviction Should Be Upheld," 1995. www.adl.org.

10. Quoted in Felicia Kessel, "Jackson: Twenty Five Years Later," *The Crisis*, June/July 1988, p. 20.

11. Dorothy I. Height, "Introduction to *I Have a Dream*," in *A Call to Conscience: The Landmark Speeches of Dr. Martin Luther King, Jr.*, eds. Clayborne Carson and Kris Shepard. New York: Intellectual Properties Management, 2001.

12. Fred Shuttlesworth, "Introduction to *Eulogy for the Young Victims of the Sixteenth Street Baptist Church Bombing*," in *A Call to Conscience: The Landmark Speeches of Dr. Martin Luther King, Jr.*, eds. Clayborne Carson and Kris Shepard. New York: Intellectual Properties Management, 2001.

13. Tom Wicker, "That Day in Dallas," *The Kennedy Assassination and the American Public*, eds. Bradley S. Greenberg and Edwin B. Parker. Stanford, CA: Stanford University Press, 1965.

ARTICLE 1

Segregation Now! Segregation Tomorrow! Segregation Forever!

By George C. Wallace

In 1958, democratic candidate George C. Wallace ran for governor of Alabama for the first time. His rival in the elections was Republican candidate John Patterson who ran strong on the racial issue and accepted the support of the Ku Klux Klan. Wallace refused support from the racist hate group and received the endorsement of the National Association for the Advancement of Colored People (NAACP). In the runoff, Patterson defeated him by over sixty-four thousand votes.

This devastating loss forced Wallace to significantly adapt his sociopolitical ideologies to appeal to the state's voters. One of the ways that Wallace improved his racist credentials was to recruit Asa Earl Carter as his main speechwriter in the 1962 election. Carter, the head of a Ku Klux Klan terrorist organization, was one of the most extreme racists in Alabama. Carter wrote most of Wallace's speeches during the campaign and this included the slogan delivered on January 14, 1963, in his inaugural address, "Segregation now! Segregation tomorrow! Segregation forever!" Carter painted desegration policies as just one more way in which the federal government was depriving states of their inherent rights and moving the nation closer to communism.

George C. Wallace, inaugural address, Montgomery, Alabama, January 14, 1963.

While serving as governor, Wallace focused on the preservation of segregation. He disagreed that the passage of a civil rights bill would alleviate the plight of African Americans. In 1963, Wallace became a mouthpiece for segregationists in the South and earned national media attention for his attempts to stop the integration of the Alabama public school system. His acts of defiance added to a terribly tense environment that was made worse by racial violence and President John F. Kennedy's attempts to force Governor Wallace to comply with federal legislation.

Today I have stood, where once Jefferson Davis [president of the Confederacy] stood, and took an oath to my people. It is very appropriate then that from this Cradle of the Confederacy, this very Heart of the Great Anglo-Saxon Southland, that today we sound the drum for freedom as have our generations of forebears before us done, time and time again through history. Let us rise to the call of freedom-loving blood that is in us and send our answer to the tyranny that clanks its chains upon the South. In the name of the greatest people that have ever trod this earth, I draw the line in the dust and toss the gauntlet before the feet of tyranny . . . and I say segregation today, segregation tomorrow, segregation forever.

Alabama Will Not Integrate Its Schools

The Washington, D.C. school riot report is disgusting and revealing. We will not sacrifice our children to any such type school system—and you can write that down. The federal troops in Mississippi could be better used guarding the safety of the citizens of Washington, D.C., where it is even unsafe to walk or go to a ballgame—and that is the nation's capital. I was safer in a B-29 bomber over Japan during the war [World War II] in an air raid, than the people of Washington are walking to the White House neighborhood. A closer example is Atlanta. The city officials fawn for political reasons over school integration and *then* build barricades to stop residential integration—what hypocrisy!

Let us send this message back to Washington by our representatives who are with us today that from this day we are standing up, and the heel of tyranny does not fit the neck of an upright man, that we intend to take the offensive and carry our fight for freedom across the nation, wielding the balance of power we know we possess in the Southland, that *we*, not the insipid bloc of voters of some sections, will determine in the next election who shall sit in the White House of these United States. That from this day, from this hour, from this minute, we give the word of a race of honor that we will tolerate their boot in our face no longer . . . and let those certain judges put *that* in their opium pipes of power and smoke it for what it is worth.

A Message for the South

Hear me, Southerners! You sons and daughters who have moved north and west throughout this nation: We call on you from your native soil to join with us in national support and vote, and we know, wherever you are, away from the hearths of the Southland, that you will respond, for though you may live in the fartherest reaches of this vast country, your heart has never left Dixieland.

And you native sons and daughters of old New England's rock-ribbed patriotism, and you sturdy natives of the great Mid-West, and you descendants of the far West flaming spirit of pioneer freedom: We invite you to come and be with us, for you are of the Southern spirit and the Southern philosophy; you are Southerners too and brothers with us in our fight.

What I have said about segregation goes double this day, and what I have said to or about some federal judges goes *triple* this day.

The Future of Alabama

Alabama has been blessed by God as few states in this Union have been blessed. Our state owns ten percent of all the natural resources of all the states in our country. Our inland waterway system is second to none and has the potential of being the greatest waterway transport system in the entire world. We possess over thirty minerals in usable quantities and our soil is rich and varied, suited to a wide variety of plants. Our native pine and forestry system produces timber faster than we can cut it and yet we have only pricked the surface of the great lumber and pulp potential.

With ample rainfall and rich grasslands our livestock industry is in the infancy of a giant future that can make us a center of the big and growing meat packing and prepared foods marketing. We have the favorable climate, streams, woodlands, beaches, and natural beauty to make us a recreational mecca in the booming tourist and vacation industry. . . .

And while the manufacturing industries of free enterprise have been coming to our state in increasing numbers, attracted by our bountiful natural resouces, our growing numbers of skilled workers and our favorable conditions, their present rate of settlement here can be increased from the trickle they now represent to a stream of enterprise and endeavor, capital and expansion that can join us in our work of development and enrichment of the educational futures of our children, the opportunities of our citizens and the fulfillment of our talents as God has given them to us.

The Threat to States' Rights

To realize our ambitions and to bring to fruition our dreams, we as Alabamians must take cognizance of the world about us. We must re-define our heritage, re-school our thoughts in the lessons our forefathers knew so well, first hand, in order to function and to grow and to prosper. We can no longer hide our head in the sand and tell ourselves that the ideology of our free fathers is not being attacked and is not being threatened by another idea . . . for it is. We are faced with an idea that if a centralized government assume enough authority, enough power over its people, that it can provide a utopian life; that if given the power to dictate, to forbid, to require, to demand, to distribute, to edict and to judge what is best and enforce that will produce only "good" . . . and it shall be our father and our God. It is an idea of government that encourages our fears and destroys our faith, for where there is faith, there is no fear, and where there is fear, there is no faith. In encouraging our fears of economic insecurity it demands we place that economic management and control with government; in encouraging our fear of educational development it demands we place that education and the minds of our children under management and control of government, and even in feeding our fears of physical infirmities and declining years, it offers and demands to father us through it all and even into the grave. It is a government that claims to us that it is bountiful as it buys its power from us with the fruits of its rapaciousness of the wealth that free men before it have produced and builds on crumbling credit without responsibilities to the debtors . . . our children. It is an ideology of government erected on the encouragement of fear and fails to recognize the basic law of our fathers that governments do not produce wealth, people produce wealth

. . . free people; and those people become less free as they learn there is little reward for ambition; that it requires faith to risk . . . and they have none . . . as the government must restrict and penalize and tax incentive and endeavor and must increase its expenditures of bounties, then this government must assume more and more police powers and we find we are become government-fearing people. . . .

A Rewriting of the Constitution Is in Progress

It is this theory of international power politic that led a group of men on the Supreme Court for the first time in American history to issue an edict, based not on legal precedent, but upon a volume, the editor of which said our Constitution is outdated and must be changed and the writers of which, some had admittedly belonged to as many as half a hundred communist-front organizations. It is this theory that led this same group of men to briefly bare the ungodly core of that philosophy in forbidding little school children to say a prayer. And we find the evidence of that ungodliness even in the removal of the words "in God we trust" from some of our dollars, which was placed there as like evidence by our founding fathers as the faith upon which this system of government was built. It is the spirit of power thirst that caused a President in Washington to take up Caesar's pen and with one stroke of it make a law. A law which the law making body of Congress refused to pass . . . a law that tells us that we can or cannot buy or sell our very homes, except by his conditions . . . and except at *his* discretion. It is the spirit of power thirst that led the same President to launch a full offensive of twenty-five thousand troops against a university . . . of all places . . . in his own country, and against his own people, when this nation maintains only six thousand troops in the beleagured city of [West] Berlin. We have witnessed such acts of "might makes right" over the world as men yielded to the temptation to play God, but we have never before witnessed it in America. We reject such acts as free men. We do not defy, for there is nothing to defy, since as free men we do not recognize any government right to give freedom or deny freedom. No government erected by man has that right. As Thomas Jefferson said, "The God who gave us life, gave us liberty at the same time; no King holds the right of liberty in his hands." Nor does any ruler in American government.

Intention to Assert States' Rights

We intend, quite simply, to practice the free heritage as bequeathed to us as sons of free fathers. We intend to re-vitalize the truly new and progressive form of government that is less than two hundred years old, a government first founded in this nation simply and purely on faith that there is a personal God who rewards good and punishes evil, that hard work will receive its just deserts, that ambition and ingenuity and incentiveness and profit of such are admirable traits and goals, that the individual is encouraged in his spiritual growth and from that growth arrives at a character that enhances his charity toward others and from that character and that charity so is influenced business, and labor and farmer and government. We intend to renew our faith as God-fearing men, *not* government-fearing men nor any other kind of fearing-men. We intend to roll up our sleeves and pitch in to develop this full bounty God has given us to live full and useful lives and in absolute freedom from all fear. Then can we enjoy the full richness of the Great American Dream.

We have placed this sign, "In God We Trust," upon our State Capitol on this Inauguration Day as physical evidence of determination to renew the faith of our fathers and to practice the free heritage they bequeathed to us. We do this with the clear and solemn knowledge that such physical evidence is evidently a direct violation of the logic of that Supreme Court in Washington, D.C., and if they or their spokesmen in this state wish to term this defiance, I say then let them make the most of it.

This nation was never meant to be a unit of one but a united of the many; that is the exact reason our freedom loving forefathers established the states, so as to divide the rights and powers among the states, insuring that no central power could gain master government control. . . .

Segregation Has a Valid Place

And so it was meant in our racial lives . . . each race, within its own framework has the freedom to teach, to instruct, to develop, to ask for and receive deserved help from others of separate racial stations. This is the great freedom of our American founding fathers, but if we amalgamate into the one unit as advocated by the communist philosophers, then the enrichment of our lives, the freedom for our development, is gone forever. We become, therefore, a mongrel unit of one under a single all powerful government, and we stand for everything and for nothing.

The true brotherhood of America, of respecting the separateness of others and uniting in effort has been so twisted and distorted from its original concept that there is a small wonder that communism is winning the world.

We invite the negro citizen of Alabama to work with us from his separate racial station, as we will work with him, to develop, to grow in individual freedom and enrichment. We want jobs and a good future for *both* races, the tubercular and the infirm. This is the basic heritage of my religion, if which I make full practice, for we are all the handiwork of God.

But we warn those, of any group, who would follow the false doctrine of communistic amalgamation that we will not surrender our system of government, our freedom of race and religion, that freedom was won at a hard price and if it requires a hard price to retain it, we are able and quite willing to pay it.

Gideon v. Wainwright and the Right to Legal Counsel

Part I by Clarence Earl Gideon;
Part II by Hugo Lafayette Black

In October 1961, Clarence Earl Gideon, was arrested on the charge of petty theft for stealing money and property from a Florida pool hall. Gideon, having no money to hire an attorney, requested that the court appoint him one in his defense. The Florida judge at the pretrial hearing denied his request stating that, under Florida law, only defendants who were charged with capital crimes could be appointed an attorney. This law was based on a previous Supreme Court ruling, the case of *Betts v. Brady*, in which the Court maintained that states did not have to appoint legal counsel to a defendant who is not being tried for capital crimes.

Gideon was a man who, with little education or money, was subsequently forced to defend himself in court. During his trial, he was unable to address certain discrepancies in his case and was ultimately convicted. When Gideon was sent to prison, he filed a habeas corpus petition. A writ of habeas corpus is a judicial mandate to a prison official ordering that an inmate be brought to the court to determine whether or not that person is imprisoned lawfully and whether or not

Part I: Clarence Earl Gideon, petitions submitted to the Supreme Court of the state of Florida, October 1961. Part II: Hugo Lafayette Black, opinion, *Gideon v. Wainwright*, 372 U.S. 335-352, 1963.

he should be released from custody. The petition must show that the court ordering the detention or imprisonment made a legal or factual error. The state of Florida's high court refused to review the case, upholding the lower court's decision. Gideon then refiled the writ with the Supreme Court of the United States in January 1962.

The Court agreed to hear his case, and appointed Florida attorney Abe Fortas to represent him. The Supreme Court found Gideon innocent, overruling the case of *Betts v. Brady*. Now, defendants had the right to an attorney that the states must provide in cases involving any possible imprisonment, however minor the offense. Federal criminal defendants had had this right for many years, but the case of *Gideon v. Wainwright* extended those rights to the state level.

Part I of the following selection is the writ of habeas corpus that Gideon submitted to the Supreme Court. Part II of the selection consists of the official Supreme Court decision for overturning Gideon's case and establishing the constitutional right for court-appointed legal representation. On March 18, 1963, the opinion of the Court was delivered by Justice Hugo Lafayette Black, a justice known for his adherence to the literal meaning of the Constitution.

After Gideon's case was overturned, he was offered a new trial with court-appointed legal representation and was acquitted of his crime.

I

I, Clarence Earl Gideon, being duly sworn according to law, depose and say that I am the above petitioner in the above-entitled cause, and, in support of my application for leave to proceed without being required to prepay costs or fees state:

1. Because of my poverty I am unable to pay cost of said cause.
2. I am unable to give security for the same.
3. I believe I am entitled to the redress I seek in said cause.
4. The nature of said cause is briefly stated as follows:

I was sentenced to the State Penitentiary by the Circuit Court of Bay County, State of Florida. The present proceeding was commenced on a petition for a Writ of Habeus Corpus to the Supreme Court of the State of Florida to vacate the sentence, on the grounds that I was made to stand trial without the aid of counsel, and, at all times of my incarceration. The said Court refused to appoint counsel and therefore deprived me of due process of law; and violated my rights in the Bill of Rights and the constitution of the United States.

CLARENCE EARL GIDEON,
Petitioner.

Petition for a Writ of Certiorari

Comes now the petitioner, Clarence Earl Gideon, a citizen of the United States of America, in proper person, and appearing as his own counsel. Who petitions this Honorable Court for a Writ of Certiorari [review of a lower court's ruling] directed to the Supreme Court of the State of Florida. To review the order and Judgement of the court below denying the petitioner a writ of Habeus Corpus.

Petitioner submits that the Supreme Court of the United States has the authority and jurisdiction to review the final Judgment of the Supreme Court of the State of Florida the highest court of the State under sec. 344(B) Title 28 U.S.C.A., and Because the "Due process clause" of the fourteenth amendment of the constitution and the fifth and sixth articles of the Bill of rights has been violated. Furthermore, the decision of the court below denying the petitioner a Writ of Habeus Corpus is also inconsistent and adverse to its own previous decisions in paralled cases.

Attached hereto, and made a part of this petition is a true copy of the petition for a Writ of Habeus Corpus as presented to the Florida Supreme Court. Petitioner asks this Honorable Court to consider the same arguments and authorities cited in the petition for Writ of Habeus Corpus before the Florida Supreme Court. In consideration of this petition for a Writ of Certiorari.

The Supreme Court of Florida did not write any opinion. Order of that Court denying petition for Writ of Habeus Corpus dated October 30, 1961, are attached hereto and made a part of this petition.

Petitioner contends that he has been deprived of due process of law Habeus Corpus petition alleging that the lower state court has decided a federal question of substance in a way not in accord with the applicable decisions of this Honorable Court. When at the time of the petitioner's trial he ask the lower court for the aid of counsel. The court refused this aid. Petitioner told the court that this court had made decision to the effect that all citizens tried for a felony crime should have aid of counsel. The lower court ignored this plea.

Petitioner alleges that prior to petitioner's convictions and sentence for Breaking and Entering with the intent to commit petty Larceny, he had requested aid of counsel, that, at the time of his conviction and sentence, petitioner was without aid of counsel. That the Court refused and did not appoint counsel, and that he was incapable adequately of making his own defense. In consequence of which he was made to stand trial. Made a Prima Facia showing of denial of due process of law. (U.S.C.A. Const. Amend. 14) *William V. Kaiser* vs. *State of Missouri,* 65 ct. 363 *Counsel must be assigned to the accused if he is unable to employ one, and incapable adequately of making his own defense. Tomkins* vs. *State Missouri,* 65 ct. 370.

On the 3rd June 1961 A.D. your Petitioner was arrested for foresaid crime and convicted for same. Petitioner receive trial and sentence without aid of counsel, your petitioner was deprived Due process of law!

Petitioner was deprived of due process of law in the court below. Evidence in the lower court did not show that a crime of Breaking and Entering with the intent to commit Petty Larceny had been committed. Your petitioner was compelled to make his own defense, he was incapable adequately of making his own defense. Petitioner did not plead nol contender But that is what his trial amounted to.

Wherefore the premises considered it is respectfully contented that the decision of the court below was in error and the case should be reviewed by this court, accordingly the writ prepared and prayed for should be issue.

It is respectfully submitted,
CLARENCE EARL GIDEON

II

Petitioner [Clarence Gideon] was charged in a Florida state court with having broken and entered a poolroom with intent to commit a misdemeanor. This offense is a felony under Florida law. Appearing in court without funds and without a lawyer, petitioner asked the court to appoint counsel for him, whereupon the following colloquy took place:

"The COURT: Mr. Gideon, I am sorry, but I cannot appoint Counsel to represent you in this case. Under the laws of the State of Florida, the only time the Court can appoint Counsel to represent a Defendant is when that person is charged with a capital offense. I am sorry, but I will have to deny your request to appoint Counsel to defend you in this case.

"The DEFENDANT: The United States Supreme Court says I am entitled to be represented by Counsel."

Put to trial before a jury, Gideon conducted his defense about as well as could be expected from a layman. He made an opening statement to the jury, cross-examined the State's witnesses, presented witnesses in his own defense, declined to testify himself, and made a short argument "emphasizing his innocence to the charge contained in the Information filed in this case." The jury returned a verdict of guilty, and petitioner was sentenced to serve five years in the state prison. Later, petitioner filed in the Florida Supreme Court this habeas corpus petition attacking his conviction and sentence on the ground that the trial court's refusal to appoint counsel for him denied him rights "guaranteed by the Constitution and the Bill of Rights by the United States Government." Treating the petition for habeas corpus as properly before it, the State Supreme Court, "upon consideration thereof" but without an opinion, denied all relief. Since 1942, when *Betts* v. *Brady*, was decided by a divided Court, the problem of a defendant's federal constitutional right to counsel in a state court has been a continuing source of controversy and litigation in both state and federal courts. To give this problem another review here, we granted certiorari [review a lower court's ruling]. Since Gideon was proceeding *in forma pauperis* [without paying legal fees, due to poverty], we appointed counsel to represent him and requested both sides to discuss in their briefs and oral arguments the following: "Should this Court's holding in *Betts* v. *Brady*, be reconsidered?"

Reviewing *Betts* v. *Brady*

The facts upon which Betts claimed that he had been unconstitutionally denied the right to have counsel appointed to assist him are strikingly like the facts upon which Gideon here bases his federal constitutional claim. Betts was indicted for robbery in a Maryland state court. On arraignment, he told the trial judge of his lack of funds to hire a lawyer and asked the court to appoint one for him. Betts was advised that it was not the practice in that county to appoint counsel for indigent defendants except in murder and rape cases. He then pleaded not guilty, had witnesses summoned, cross-examined the State's witnesses, examined his own, and chose not to testify himself. He was found guilty by the judge, sitting without a jury, and sentenced to eight years in prison. Like Gideon, Betts sought release by habeas corpus, alleging that he had been denied the right to assistance of counsel in violation of the Fourteenth Amendment. Betts was denied any relief, and on review this Court affirmed. It was held that a refusal to appoint counsel for an indigent defendant charged with a felony did not necessarily violate the Due Process Clause of the Fourteenth Amendment, which for reasons given the Court deemed to be the only applicable federal constitutional provision. The Court said:

> "Asserted denial [of due process] is to be tested by an appraisal of the totality of facts in a given case. That which may, in one setting, constitute a denial of fundamental fairness, shocking to the universal sense of justice, may, in other circumstances, and in the light of other considerations, fall short of such denial."

Treating due process as "a concept less rigid and more fluid than those envisaged in other specific and particular provisions of the Bill of Rights," the Court held that refusal to appoint counsel under the particular facts and circumstances in the *Betts* case was not so "offensive to the common and fundamental ideas of fairness" as to amount to a denial of due process. Since the facts and circumstances of the two cases are so nearly indistinguishable, we think the *Betts* v. *Brady* holding if left standing would require us to reject Gideon's claim that the Constitution guarantees him the assistance of counsel. Upon full reconsideration we conclude that *Betts* v. *Brady* should be overruled.

Reasons for the *Betts* v. *Brady* Ruling

The Sixth Amendment provides, "In all criminal prosecutions, the accused shall enjoy the right . . . to have the Assistance of Counsel for his defence." We have construed this to mean that in federal courts counsel must be provided for defendants unable to employ counsel unless the right is competently and intelligently waived. Betts argued that this right is extended to indigent defendants in state courts by the Fourteenth Amendment. In response the Court stated that, while the Sixth Amendment laid down "no rule for the conduct of the States, the question recurs whether the constraint laid by the Amendment upon the national courts expresses a rule so fundamental and essential to a fair trial, and so, to due process of law, that it is made obligatory upon the States by the Fourteenth Amendment." In order to decide whether the Sixth Amendment's guarantee of counsel is of this fundamental nature, the Court in *Betts* set out and considered "[r]elevant data on the subject . . . afforded by constitutional and statutory provisions subsisting in the colonies and the States prior to the inclusion of the Bill of Rights in the national Constitution, and in the constitutional, legislative, and judicial history of the States to the present date." On the basis of this historical data the Court concluded that "appointment of counsel is not a fundamental right, essential to a fair trial." It was for this reason the *Betts* Court refused to accept the contention that the Sixth Amendment's guarantee of counsel for indigent federal defendants was extended to or, in the words of that Court, "made obligatory upon the States by the Fourteenth Amendment." Plainly, had the Court concluded that appointment of counsel for an indigent criminal defendant was "a fundamental right, essential to a fair trial," it would have held that the Fourteenth Amendment requires appointment of counsel in a state court, just as the Sixth Amendment requires in a federal court.

Rethinking *Betts* v. *Brady*

We think the Court in *Betts* had ample precedent for acknowledging that those guarantees of the Bill of Rights which are fundamental safeguards of liberty immune from federal abridgment are equally protected against state invasion by the Due Process Clause of the Fourteenth Amendment. This same principle was recognized, explained, and applied in *Powell* v. *Alabama* (1932), a case upholding the right of counsel, where the Court held that despite sweeping language to the contrary in *Hurtado* v. *California* (1884), the Fourteenth Amendment "embraced" those "'fundamental principles of liberty and justice which lie at the base of all our civil and political institutions,'" even though they had been "specifically dealt with in another part of the federal Constitution." In many cases other than *Powell* and *Betts*, this Court has looked to the fundamental nature of original Bill of Rights guarantees to decide whether the Fourteenth Amendment makes them obligatory on the States. Explicitly recognized to be of this "fundamental nature" and therefore made immune from state invasion by the Fourteenth, or some part of it, are the First Amendment's freedoms of speech, press, religion, assembly, association, and petition for redress of grievances. For the same reason, though not always in precisely the same terminology, the Court has made obligatory on the States the Fifth Amendment's command that private property shall not be taken for public use without just compensation, the Fourth Amendment's prohibition of unreasonable searches and seizures, and the Eighth's ban on cruel and unusual punishment. On the other hand, this Court in *Palko* v. *Connecticut* (1937), refused to hold that the Fourteenth Amendment made the double jeopardy provision of the Fifth Amendment obligatory on the States. In so refusing, however, the Court, speaking through Mr. Justice Cardozo, was careful to emphasize that "immunities that are valid as against the federal government by force of the specific pledges of particular amendments have been found to be implicit in the concept of ordered liberty, and thus, through the Fourteenth Amendment, become valid as against the states" and that guarantees "in their origin . . . effective against the federal government alone" had by prior cases "been taken over from the earlier articles of the federal bill of rights and brought within the Fourteenth Amendment by a process of absorption."

The Right to Counsel Is Fundamental

We accept *Betts* v. *Brady*'s assumption, based as it was on our prior cases, that a provision of the Bill of Rights which is "fundamental and essential to a fair trial" is made obligatory upon the States by the Fourteenth Amendment. We think the Court in *Betts* was wrong, however, in concluding that the Sixth Amendment's guarantee of counsel is not one of these fundamental rights. Ten years before *Betts* v. *Brady*, this Court, after full consideration of all the historical data examined in *Betts*, had unequivocally declared that "the right of the aid of counsel is of this fundamental character." *Powell* v. *Alabama* (1932). While the Court at the close of its *Powell* opinion did by its language, as this Court frequently does, limit its holding to the particular facts and circumstances of that case, its conclusions about the fundamental nature of the right to counsel are unmistakable. Several years later, in 1936, the Court reemphasized what it had said about the fundamental nature of the right to counsel in this language:

"We concluded that certain fundamental rights, safeguarded by the first eight amendments against federal action, were also safeguarded against state action by the due process of law clause of the Fourteenth Amendment, and among them the fundamental right of the accused to the aid of counsel in a criminal prosecution." *Grosjean* v. *American Press Co.*

And again in 1938 this Court said:

"[The assistance of counsel] is one of the safeguards of the Sixth Amendment deemed necessary to insure fundamental human rights of life and liberty. . . . The Sixth Amendment stands as a constant admonition that if the constitutional safeguards it provides be lost, justice will not 'still be done.'" *Johnson* v. *Zerbst.*

Attorneys Are Essential Trial Elements

In light of these and many other prior decisions of this Court, it is not surprising that the *Betts* Court, when faced with the contention that "one charged with crime, who is unable to obtain counsel, must be furnished counsel by the State," concede that "[e]xpressions in the opinions of this court lend color to the argument. . . ." The fact is that in deciding as it did—that "appointment of counsel is not a fundamental right, essential to a fair trial"—the Court in *Betts* v. *Brady* made an abrupt break with its own well-considered precedents. In returning to these old precedents, sounder we believe than the new, we but restore constitutional principles established to achieve a fair system of justice. Not only these precedents but also reason and reflection require us to recognize that in our adversary system of criminal justice, any person haled into court, who is too poor to hire a lawyer, cannot be assured a fair trial unless counsel is provided for him. This seems to us to be an obvious truth. Governments, both state and federal, quite properly spend vast sums of money to establish machinery to try defendants accused of crime. Lawyers to prosecute are everywhere deemed essential to protect the public's interest in an orderly society. Similarly, there are few defendants charged with crime, few indeed, who fail to hire the best lawyers they can get to prepare and present their defenses. That government hires lawyers to prosecute and defendants who have the money hire lawyers to defend are the strongest indications of the widespread belief that lawyers in criminal courts are necessities, not luxuries. The right of one charged with crime to counsel may not be deemed fundamental and essential to fair trials in some countries, but it is in ours. From the very beginning, our state and national constitutions and laws have laid great emphasis on procedural and substantive safeguards designed to assure fair trials before impartial tribunals in which every defendant stands equal before the law. This noble ideal cannot be realized if the poor man charged with crime has to face his accusers without a lawyer to assist him. A defendant's need for a lawyer is nowhere better stated than in the moving words of Mr. Justice Sutherland in *Powell* v. *Alabama:*

> "The right to be heard would be, in many cases, of little avail if it did not comprehend the right to be heard by counsel. Even the intelligent and educated layman has small and sometimes no skill in the science of law. If charged with crime, he is incapable, generally, of determining for himself whether the indictment is good or bad. He is unfamiliar with the rules of evidence. Left without the aid of counsel he may be put on trial without a proper charge, and convicted upon incompetent evidence, or evidence irrelevant to the issue or otherwise inadmissible. He lacks both the skill and knowledge adequately to prepare his defense, even though he have a perfect one. He requires the guiding hand of counsel at every step in the proceeding against him. Without it, though he be not guilty, he faces the danger of conviction because he does not know how to establish his innocence."

Betts v. *Brady* Is Overturned

The Court in *Betts* v. *Brady* departed from the sound wisdom upon which the Court's holding in *Powell* v. *Alabama* rested. Florida, supported by two other States, has asked that *Betts* v. *Brady* be left intact. Twenty-two States, as friends of the Court, argue that *Betts* was "an anachronism when handed down" and that it should now be overruled. We agree.

The judgment is reversed and the cause is remanded to the Supreme Court of Florida for further action not inconsistent with this opinion.

The Feminine Mystique and the Feminist Movement

By Daniel Horowitz

Betty Friedan's role as a leader of the feminist movement of the 1960s began with her book, *The Feminine Mystique.* For her fifteenth Smith College reunion in 1957 she sent questionnaires to members of her class asking them to describe their lives since college. The majority replied, stating they had been married and had several children. Most of these bright, educated women expressed a sense of dissatisfaction with these roles and said that they wanted a more fulfilling function in society. From their answers and other research came the book *The Feminine Mystique*, which Friedan published in 1963. It was an instant best-seller, was excerpted in major women's magazines, and made Friedan an instant celebrity. Friedan's book effectively argued that sub-urban middle-class women were not necessarily fulfilled by their roles as housewives and mothers. She also effectively made the case that women were as capable of performing most, if not all, of the job functions that men currently performed in society, and that women would rather find fulfillment in these roles. She criticized psychiatrists, social scientists, educators, and businessmen who foisted traditional feminine roles upon the public and thereby encouraged women to live unfulfilling lives.

In 1966, Friedan helped found the National Organization for Women (NOW). As president during its first three years, she wrote

Daniel Horowitz, *Betty Friedan and the Making of the Feminine Mystique.* Amherst: University of Massachusetts Press, 1998. Copyright © 1998 by the University of Massachusetts Press. Reproduced by permission.

NOW's founding statement demanding full equality for women in the mainstream of American life. During her tenure as NOW's leader, she also led the organization in its decision to support the Equal Rights Amendment (ERA) for women and pushed for legalized abortion. During her presidency, she traveled across the country lecturing on the topic of new feminism. In this selection from his book *Betty Friedan and the Making of the Feminine Mystique*, biographer Daniel Horowitz examines the impact of Friedan's book on the emerging women's movement and explains the importance of Friedan in motivating women to push for equal rights in a male-dominated society.

It has become commonplace to see the publication of Betty Friedan's *The Feminine Mystique* in 1963 as a major turning point in the history of modern American feminism and, more generally, in the history of the postwar period. And with good reason, for her book was a key factor in the revival of the women's movement and in the transformation of the nation's awareness of the challenges middle-class suburban women faced. *The Feminine Mystique* helped millions of women comprehend, and then change, the conditions of their lives. The book took already familiar ideas, made them easily accessible, and gave them a forceful immediacy. It explored issues that others had articulated but failed to connect with women's experiences—the meaning of American history, the nature of alienated labor, the existence of the identity crisis, the threat of atomic warfare, the implications of Nazi anti-Semitism, the use of psychology as Cultural criticism, and the dynamics of sexuality. By extending to women many of the ideas about the implications of affluence that widely read male authors had developed for white, middle-class men, Friedan's book not only stood as an important endpoint in the development of 1950s social criticism but also translated that tradition into feminist terms. In addition, the book raises questions about the trajectory of Friedan's ideology, specifically about the relationship between her labor radicalism of the 1940s and early 1950s and her feminism in the 1960s.

To connect a book to a life is no easy matter. Although Friedan herself has emphasized the importance of the questionnaires her Smith [college for women] classmates filled out during the spring of 1957, when she was thirty-six years old, she also acknowledged in 1976 that in writing *The Feminine Mystique* "all the pieces of my own life came together for the first time." Here she was on the mark. It is impossible for someone to have come out of nowhere, and in so short a time, to the deep understanding of women's lives that Friedan offered in 1963. Experiences from her childhood in Peoria, her analysis of the Smith questionnaire, and all points in between, helped shape the 1963 book. . . .

Popular Feminism vs. Friedan's Perspective

The discussions of women's issues in Old Left circles beginning in the 1940s and Friedan's 1963 book had a good deal in common. They both offered wide-ranging treatments of the forces arrayed against women—the media, education, and professional expertise. Progressive women in the 1940s and Friedan in 1963 explored the alienating nature of housework. They showed an awareness of male chauvinism but ultimately lay the blame at the door of capitalism. They saw *Modern Woman: The Lost Sex* as the text that helped launch the anti-feminist attack. . . .

Yet despite these similarities, the differences between Popular Front feminism and *The Feminine Mystique* were considerable. In articulating a middle-class, suburban feminism, Friedan both drew on and repudiated her Popular Front feminism. What happened in Friedan's life between 1953, when she last published an article on working women in the labor press, and 1963, when her book on suburban women appeared, fundamentally shaped *The Feminine Mystique.* Over time, a series of events undermined Friedan's hopes that male-led radical social movements would fight for women with the consistency and dedication she felt necessary. Disillusioned and chastened by the male chauvinism in unions but also by the [Atomic] Bomb, the Holocaust, the Cold War, and McCarthyism [the era of Communist persecution led by Senator Joe McCarthy], she turned elsewhere. Her therapy in the mid-1950s enabled her to rethink her past and envision her future.

Always a writer who worked with the situations and material close at hand, in the early 1950s Friedan began to apply what she learned about working-class women in progressive feminist discussions of the 1940s to the situation that middle-class women faced in suburbs. Living in Parkway Village and Rockland County at the same time she was writing for the [liberal newspaper] *Parkway Villager* and mass-circulation magazines, Friedan had begun to describe how middle-class and wealthy women worked against great odds to achieve and grow. What she wrote about democratic households and cooperative communities, as well as her long-held dream of the satisfactions that romance and marriage would provide, reflected her high hopes for what life in the suburbs might bring. Although she felt that in the mid-1950s she successfully broke through the strictures of the feminine mystique she would describe in her 1963 book, the problems with her marriage and suburban life fostered in her a disillusionment different from but in many ways more profound than what she had experienced with the sexual politics of the Popular Front.

The Connection to Early Writings

If all these experiences provided a general background out of which her 1963 book emerged, the more proximate origins of *The Feminine Mystique* lay in what she focused on during her career as a free-lance writer. She well understood the connection between the magazine articles she began to publish in the mid-1950s and her 1963 book. In addition, a critical impetus to her book was her response to McCarthyism. When she drew on her 1952 survey of her classmates to write "Was Their Education UnAmerican?" she first gave evidence of pondering the relationship between her Smith education, the struggle for civil liberties, and what it meant for women to thrive as thinkers and public figures in the suburbs. Then in her work on Intellectual Resources Pool, which began about the same time that she looked over those fateful questionnaires, Friedan paid sustained attention to the question of what it meant for middle-class women to develop an identity in American suburbs, including an identity as intellectuals. She asked these questions at a time when the whole culture, but especially anti-communists, seemed to be conspiring to suppress not only the vitality of intellectual life for which free speech was so important but also the aspirations of educated women to achieve a full sense of themselves. . . .

Early Attempts to Market Her Work

The magazine editors who in 1962 looked at articles derived from Friedan's book chapters raised questions about the scope, tone, and originality of her work. Some of their comments prefigured the anti-feminist diatribes that came with the book's publication in 1963. The editors at *Reporter* [a popular news journal] found Friedan's chapters "too shrill and humorless." A male editor from *Redbook* turned down one excerpt from the book, saying it was "heavy going," and another for expressing "a rather strident" perspective. "Put us down as a group of smug or evil males," remarked an editor of *Antioch Review* [a literary magazine], who found that Friedan's chapter "The Sexual Sell" "contributes little to understanding or solution of the problems it raises." Friedan's article, he concluded, was "dubious sociology which attempts to answer too much with too little.". . .

Friedan faced the problem of positioning her book in what she and her editors saw as an increasingly crowded field of writings on middle-class women. Although we tend to see *The Feminine Mystique* as a book that stands by itself, Friedan and her publisher were aware that others had already articulated many of the book's concerns. When a vice president of [book publisher] W.W. Norton wrote [author] Pearl S. Buck to solicit a jacket blurb, he remarked that "one of our problems is that much is being written these days about the plight (or whatever it is) of the educated American woman; therefore, this one will have to fight its way out of a thicket.". . .

There were additional indications that Friedan was racing against the clock. While the book gave some the impression of a powerful and unshakable feminine mystique, Friedan herself acknowledged in the book that around 1960 the media began to pay attention to the discontents of middle-class American women. There is plenty of evidence that Friedan's readers, from professional women to housewives, found what she had to say either familiar or less than shocking. Some of those who reviewed the book found nothing particularly new or dramatic in it. Similarly, although some women who wrote Friedan indicated that they found an intense revelatory power in her words, others said they were tired of negative writings that, they believed, belabored the women's situation.

If what Friedan wrote was hardly new to so many, then why did the book have such an impact? We can begin to answer that question by examining the ways she reworked familiar themes to give them a special urgency, especially for middle-class white women. Nowhere was this clearer than on the issue of women's work. Especially striking is the contrast between her animus [anger] against the toil of housewives and volunteers and her strong preference for women entering the paid work force, a dichotomy a friend warned her not to fall back on. Here Friedan was advocating what she had learned from labor radicals who urged women to get paying jobs and to work cooperatively with men. Friedan recast the terms of a long-standing debate between men and women so that it would appeal to middle-class readers. In her discussion of housework, for example, she offered only scattered hints about the reluctance of husbands to help with household chores. At one moment, she mentioned "the active resentment of husbands" of career women, while elsewhere she praised cooperative husbands. Neither perspective enabled her to discuss openly or fully what she felt about her marriage, the sexual politics of marriage, and the attempts by women, herself included, to set things right. As a labor journalist she had talked of oppressive factory work for working-class women; in *The Feminine Mystique*, alienated labor involved the unrecompensed efforts by white, middle-class women to keep their suburban homes spotless. One reader picked up on what it might mean, in both trivial and profound ways, to apply a Marxist analysis to suburban women. In 1963, the woman wrote to Friedan that the book made her wish to rush into streets and cry "To arms, sisters! You have nothing to lose but your vacuum cleaners.". . .

Like others, Friedan offered what the historian Ellen Herman has called a "postmaterial agenda" which employed psychological concepts to undergird feminism. Here Friedan was responding to the way writers—including Philip Wylie, Edward Strecker, Ferdinand Lundberg, and Marynia Farnham—used psychology to suggest that only the acceptance of domesticity would cure female frustrations. Friedan's contribution was to turn the argument around, asserting that women's misery came from the attempt to keep them in place. Psychology, rather than convincing women to adjust and conform, could be used to foster their personal growth and fuller embrace of non-domestic roles. Other observers suggested the troublesome nature of male identity in the 1950s; Friedan gave this theme a twist. She both recognized the problems posed by feminized men and masculinized women and went on to promise that the liberation of women would strengthen male and female identity alike. Friedan took from other writers an analysis that blamed the problems of diminished masculine identity on life in the suburbs, jobs in large organizations, and consumer culture; she then turned this explanation into an argument for women's liberation.

Down, Down, Then Silence

By Frank Trippett

The USS *Thresher* was the first of a new class of nuclear submarines designed to dive significantly deeper than its predecessors. After nearly a year of record-breaking operations, the submarine underwent a scheduled shipyard overhaul in Portsmouth, New Hampshire, that required significant alterations to its hydraulic system, the system used to propel the submarine. At the time of the overhaul, four other submarines were also undergoing significant alterations placing a strain on available materials. The *Thresher*'s overhaul was conducted under tight schedule constraints, and several of the maintenance standards were overlooked in order to complete the overhaul on time.

On the morning of April 10, 1963, the USS *Thresher* proceeded to conduct sea trials about two hundred miles off the coast of Cape Cod. At 9:13 A.M., the submarine rescue ship, USS *Skylark*, received a signal indicating that the submarine was experiencing "minor difficulties." At 9:18 A.M., the *Skylark*'s sonar picked up the sounds of the submarine breaking apart. All 129 crew members were lost in what is considered one of the worst naval disasters in U.S. history.

The navy's investigation concluded that while the *Thresher* was operating at test depth, a leak had developed in an engine room's seawater system, and water from the leak may have short-circuited electrical equipment, causing a reactor shutdown, leaving the submarine without primary and secondary propulsion systems. The submarine was unable to blow its main ballast tanks, and because of the boat's

Frank Trippett, "Down, Down, Then Silence," *Newsweek*, vol. LX, April 22, 1963, pp. 26–28.

weight and depth, the power available from the emergency propulsion motor was insufficient to propel the submarine to the surface. After the investigation, the navy embarked on an extensive review of practices and procedures in effect during the *Thresher*'s overhaul. The reviewers determined that existing standards at the time were not followed throughout the refit to ensure safe operation of the submarine.

Frank Trippett is a journalist who worked for the Fredericksburg (Virginia) *Free Lance-Star*, and was the Capital Bureau Chief for the St. Petersburg (Florida) *Times* before joining *Newsweek* magazine as an associate editor in 1961. He later became a senior editor at *Look* magazine and a senior writer and essayist for *Time* magazine during the latter sixties.

S he was the U.S.S. Thresher, named for a shark, and styled for attack with a shark-shaped hull. First of a new class of atomic submarines, the Thresher was the world's fastest moving and deepest diving undersea craft, a blue-black $45 million precision war machine, and this was Rear Adm. L.R. Daspit, commander of the Atlantic submarine force, paying tribute at her launching in Portsmouth, N.H., three years ago. Her great promise was short-lived.

On a test run after nine months of overhaul, the Thresher plunged to the bottom of the Atlantic Ocean last week, carrying with her 129 men—16 officers, 96 enlisted men, and 17 civilians. She also carried with her a young legend of invulnerability. And she left behind a bottomless mystery: how did it happen? It was the worst submarine disaster in history,[1] the first to strike any of the U.S.'s 30 atomic-powered underwater craft. Somehow the grief was more poignant because the riddle of the Thresher's fate might never be fathomed.

What was definitely known was starkly, frustratingly skimpy. At 8 A.M. Wednesday some 220 miles east of Boston, Lt. Comdr. John W. Harvey, Annapolis-trained skipper of the Thresher since January, began putting his 278-foot-long and 3,700-ton craft through her paces—routine stuff, the Navy said, a standard shakedown testing the boat's fitness after 130 structural modifications in the drydock at Portsmouth, N.H. On the previous day, the first out, Harvey had run through shallow dives and reported

---

1. Highest previous toll: 102 dead when the U.S.S. Argonant was lost in the Pacific in 1943.

no trouble. Wednesday, raw and overcast, with 40-knot winds kicking up 9-foot waves was the day for dives to maximum depths. How deep was secret; the Navy said the goal was "in excess of 400 feet," some sources put it at about 1,000 feet.

Harvey ordered the Thresher down. Diving and leveling, diving and leveling, the sharp-nosed sub cut unseen stairsteps in the deep. Steadily, through underwater voice phone, she reported her progress to the Skylark, a submarine rescue ship overseeing the tests from the surface. At 9:13 the Thresher calmly reported "minor difficulties" and said she was trying to blow out her air tanks to surface. Then, at 9:17, another message reached the Skylark. The first words were garbled, but the last two, according to Lt. (j.g.) James D. Watson, Skylark navigator, were clear: "test depth." "Shortly after that," Watson testified at the weekend, "[we] heard a sound that registered with me as being familiar from World War II. It sounded as though a compartment was collapsing . . . a rather muted, dull thud." Watson said he and the Skylark commander agreed it could have been a "breaking up" sound. It was, in any event, the last contact the men in the U.S.S. Thresher ever had with the world above the sea.

Flotsam

At 11:04 A.M., when for nearly two hours the sub had not responded to the Skylark's signals—by voice phone, Morse code, and underwater explosions meaning "surface at once"—the attending ship set in motion a far-ranging air and sea search. All that later turned up, bobbing in the turbulent Atlantic, were the final mute messages from the Thresher—two oil slicks, bits of plastic and cork from the inner hull, half a dozen red and yellow gloves used by crewmen in the sub's engine room, a plastic water glass, a tube of Baker's Flavoring, evidently from the galley. The flotsam only confirmed what the Navy had reluctantly surmised—that the Thresher lay on the Atlantic floor, her men beyond hope and her 278-foot-long hull, perhaps broken in two, beyond salvage—and indeed beyond reach. She had sunk in 8,400 feet of water—enough to cover six Empire State Buildings stacked end on end.

What had gone wrong? Sabotage? Enemy Action? Atomic reactor trouble? Human error? Had the diving planes locked, sending the Thresher beyond her maximum depth to be crushed by intolerable water pressure? Had repairs and hull modifications made in drydock proved faulty? Theories proliferated; so did rumors and speculation.

No Radioactivity

By Thursday, a saddened Adm. George W. Anderson, Chief of Naval Operations, dismissed several possibilities. Sabotage was "very remote" and action by a hostile ship out of the question. Emphatically, the CNO told Pentagon reporters there was "no indication whatever" that a reactor failure caused the disaster. (With equal emphasis, the Navy denied the disaster had created any radiation hazard, and said water samples from the site showed no radioactivity.)

Elsewhere in the Pentagon, one submarine admiral summed up most other possibilities in a talk with NEWSWEEK's correspondent Lloyd Norman. "A valve could have given way," he said. "A fitting could have gone. A small flaw in the hull could have cracked open under the great pressures. The bow planes could have stuck and the submarine could have kept diving below its safe level. Mechanical or human failure could have opened a valve or a tube. It's pure speculation. Some mysteries the sea keeps to itself."

Most Navy engineers, however, leaned to the view that a defective valve fitting or human error was the "most likely" cause of the sinking.

Questions were raised, however, about workmanship at the Portsmouth shipyard, where workers recently carved a yard-square patch of steel out of the Thresher's hull to install a torpedo tube-like garbage ejection machine. But officials said the rewelded seams had been checked and rechecked, even X-rayed before final approval.

Nobody pretended to know the final answer. But before the week was out, in fact, the newly appointed five-man board of inquiry headed by Vice Adm. Bernard L. Austin, president of the Naval War College had convened in Portsmouth and begun an intensive effort to find it. The first witness, Comdr. Dean L. Axene, Harvey's predecessor as skipper of the Thresher, praised the quality of both the ship and crew, and speculated that the sinking resulted from an almost instantaneous "flooding type casualty." Board members will make detailed inspections of the Thresher's sister ships, the Tinosa and the Jack, both under construction at Portsmouth now. But the Navy held fast to its plans to construct 22 more nuclear-powered submarines like the Thresher—built for sea attack (not as Polaris missile carriers).

Eventually, the court may get the benefit of direct observation of the wreckage of the Thresher, by means of the Navy's deep-diving bathyscaphe, the Trieste (box).

As the investigation began, only one thing seemed beyond dispute. Whatever happened to the Thresher happened with paralyzing suddenness—so fast that it not only cut off ordinary communication immediately, but left the skipper no chance to trigger his submarine emergency signal—a red flare which ignites on leaving the water and wafts, burning, from a parachute. Speculating on just such an instantaneous disaster, one expert said even a microscopic crack, at great depths, could split suddenly and admit a high-speed torrent of water powerful enough to cut the submarine in two. Submariners brooded last week on such terrifying possibilities.

Disbelief

And so did the wives, mothers, and children of the Thresher submariners. Even so, relatives of the crewmen greeted Wednesday's first reports that the sub was missing with disbelief and insistent hope. "I only concede that he's missing," said Mrs. James J. Henry of Brooklyn, mother of James Henry Jr., a lieutenant junior grade aboard the sub. "But, dear God," she added, "he's not dead."

By the next day, when Navy Secretary Fred Korth formally confirmed the Thresher's fate, such doubt was no longer possible. But even then few of the crew's families—all accustomed to the threat of imminent disaster—gave way to fruitless emotion. Typically, at her home in New London, Conn., the widow of the sub's 35-year-old commanding officer displayed the quiet valor of the Navy wife: "Our men," said Irene Harvey, mother of two boys, "have been lost performing the duty they chose and their way of life, in the service of their country." She well knew her husband's love for the Navy. "It's much nicer under the water," he had said once during his nine years in the atomic sub service. "We all like it better and feel at home there."

In one family, the news of the Thresher was doubly dreadful: two brothers—Benjamin N. Shafer, 35, of Gales Ferry, Conn., and John D. Shafer, 33, of Groton, Conn.—were electricians' mates with the crew. But in Portsmouth, home of 40 families with relatives on the Thresher, grief fell on the whole town. When the news came everybody was gearing up for a big Thursday-night party in the Navy shipyard gym. It was to commemorate the 63rd anniversary of the submarine service. Instead, townfolk turned out for a memorial service in the shipyard chapel.

Amid the sadness, some gave in to bitterness (one wife said her husband, an enlisted man, had called the Thresher "a coffin" which should never have made the trip). Others could consider themselves lucky. Sonar technician James Ward of Summit, N.J., received orders to report immediately to the Thresher—but only after she left on the test cruise. Lt. Raymond McCoole missed the cruise because illness at home prompted a two-day leave, Ashen-faced, he said: "I should have been on her. She is my ship."

The tragedy also was felt around the world. Messages of condolences to the American people and the grieved families came in from Queen Elizabeth and President de Gaulle. There was a note from West Germany's President Heinrich Lübke. Another expressed the "deepest sympathy" of Premier Hayato Ikeda of Japan—where, by chance, the disaster jeopardized delicate U.S. negotiations for permission to station atomic subs at Japanese bases; the Japanese feared a radiation hazard.

It was a sorrowful but proud President Kennedy, himself a Navy hero, who spoke for the nation and ordered flags at half-staff. "This boat," he said, "pioneered a new era in the eternal drama of the sea. . . . The courage and dedication of these men . . . is no less than that of their fathers who led their advance on the frontiers of our civilization. . . . The future of our country will always be sure when there are men such as these to give their lives to preserve it."

U.S. Astronaut Orbits Earth a Record Twenty-Two Times

By L. Gordon Cooper Jr.

On May 15 and 16, while Colonel L. Gordon Cooper Jr. piloted the Mercury spacecraft *Faith 7*, he solidified the sense of hope that John Glenn's historic flight in February 1962 had done so much to renew for the American people. Cooper orbited the earth a record twenty-two times, beating the previous Russian record set by cosmonaut Gherman Titov in October 1961. The Mercury program had been a successful project for the scientists of the National Aeronautics and Space Administration (NASA) as all four of the program's manned space flights brought back important scientific evidence from their trips into space.

The Mercury program was officially canceled on June 13, 1963, due to NASA's decision to pour its resources into building a spacecraft that would carry a man to the moon, a feat that would eventually be accomplished in 1969, and would make the United States the superior frontrunner in the race for advances in space technologies.

In the following selection, Cooper gives a detailed summary of his flight and discusses the sensation of zero gravity, the beauty of the stars and the sun from space, as well as the problematic electrical failure that caused him to perform a manual reentry.

L. Gordon Cooper Jr., "Astronaut's Summary Flight Report," *Mercury Project Summary Including Results of the Fourth Manned Orbital Flight: May 15 and 16, 1963*. Washington, DC: Office of Science and Technical Information, National Aeronautics and Space Administration, 1963.

T he [Mercury spacecraft] MA-9 flight marked the conclusion to the United States' first manned space-flight program. From their initiation into the program in 1959, the seven Mercury astronauts participated as a specialist team, and their combined experiences, both in space and on the ground, constitute a valuable contribution to the nation's manned space-flight capability. The launch checkout activities constitute one of the most valuable portions of this experience, and the MA-9 flight demonstrated once again how critical this period is both to the preparation of the spacecraft and the pilot. The sensations and experiences of the flight were generally similar to those reported by the pilots of previous flights with the exception that better dark adaptation was obtained and therefore more dim light phenomena could be seen. During the MA-9 flight, the zodiacal light and what may have been the daytime airglow were observed for the first time. While some new observations were made on phenomena such as the airglow and space particles, the appearance of the earth features and weather patterns generally seemed to be similar to the description of the previous pilots. As on previous flights, several photographic studies were conducted and the results of these exercises have proved to be valuable. A series of new experiments and evaluations of Mercury systems were conducted, with generally good results. The mission appeared to be relatively routine until a malfunction in the control system late in the flight made it necessary to control attitude manually during retrofire and reentry. The flight of *Faith 7* concluded after some 34 hours in space with a landing within 4½ miles of the primary recovery ship, the *USS Kearsarge*, in the Pacific Ocean. . . .

Preflight Preparations

The period from the time the spacecraft arrived at Cape Canaveral until the time it was mated with the launch vehicle was the period where the pilot and his backup became completely familiar with the spacecraft and all its various systems. We learned all the individual idiosyncrasies of each system. We also became familiar with many of the members of the launch crew and learned whom to call on for expert advice on each system. It was also during this period that we had an opportunity to discuss the coming flight with team members who had flown before and take advantage of their experiences.

The preflight phase was used to incorporate certain modifications into the spacecraft and to add some pieces of equipment necessary to meet operational requirements. Because of the limited usable cockpit space and the even more limited center-of-gravity travel and gross weight of the Mercury spacecraft, these configuration changes were always a soul-searching problem. Regardless of how they were accomplished, additions often resulted in some type of compromise to the pilot's comfort, freedom of movement, and/ or operational smoothness.

The natural tendency was for everyone to want to improve on existing equipment and to add worthwhile experiments that could be fitted in. Space flight is so expensive that no one wants to waste a single second of orbital time. However, we all discovered that the entire flight is compromised when all equipment, all experiments, and all the flight plan detail are not frozen early enough to check out each piece of equipment and allow everyone, particularly the pilot, to become thoroughly familiar with all procedures.

On all our flights the cockpits have been cluttered to the point where the space remaining for the astronaut and the equipment with which he must work is very limited and inefficiently arranged. In most cases getting some of the equipment located and moved about provided more exercise than did the special on-board exercise device. Stowage of equipment is a very real problem that too often is not given enough consideration. . . .

Countdown to Launch

I believe that we can very readily shorten the time that the pilot is in the spacecraft prior to launch. I was busy enough with the countdown activities that time did not drag, but I did have time to take a short nap during this period. It seems to me that to conserve the pilot's energy it would be desirable to accomplish more of these checks with the backup pilot prior to insertion. Of course, you do need a few minutes to shift around and get settled, see that the equipment is located properly, before you are prepared for the flight.

Most of the countdowns in Mercury went fairly smoothly as a result of the practice that the launch crews had acquired on simulated flight tests. The first attempt to launch MA-9 on May 14 was delayed for a diesel engine that would not operate to drive the gantry back. Then it had to be postponed because a critical radar set became inoperative. I was in the cockpit for some 6 hours before we scrubbed on that first day. I was quite tired but felt ready to recycle for another count the following day.

The countdown on May 15, 1963, went almost perfectly. Everything was really in a "go" status and I think everyone felt that we were going to have a good launch. And it was! And it was!

I had thought that I would become a bit more tense as the count neared minus 1 or 2 minutes, but found that I have been more tense for the kick-off when playing football than I was for the launch on May 15. I felt that I was very well trained and was ready to fly a good flight.

Experiencing Liftoff

It is a wonderful feeling when the engines light and you have lifted off. The long period of preparation is over, and at last you are ready to settle down to your work.

The acceleration is not disconcerting or degrading at the levels encountered in the Mercury flights. In fact, it gives one somewhat the same feeling as that of adding full throttle on a fast car, or a racing boat, or a fighter airplane. The pilot can easily monitor several of the more critical parameters, including his attitudes, throughout the entire launch phase. The task that he is given to do should be uncluttered with minor details if possible, but he is fully capable of functioning as an intricate part of the system throughout the entire launch. I was surprised at how many things I could keep track of and feel that I had plenty of time to do the exact item planned. . . .

Booster engine cutoff (BECO) is very distinctive, by the decrease in both the acceleration and the noise. It was just as I had expected it to be from talking to the others.

[First astronaut to orbit the earth] John Glenn and [second astronaut to orbit the earth] Scott Carpenter had discussed with [astronaut] Wally Schirra and me how they had encountered some springboard effect from the guidance while in the latter phases of the sustainer flight. Wally Schirra experienced very little or none of this effect. I had an almost perfect sustainer trajectory with almost no guidance corrections at all, so it was an exceptionally smooth and almost perfect insertion.

Sustainer engine cutoff (SECO) is also quite distinctive, in the same manner as BECO. This is followed by the noise of clamp rings and posigrade rockets. The spacecraft is in orbit.

We had all run many full launch profiles on the centrifuge, so

I felt very well prepared for all the powered flight, but there is some difference between the transition from positive acceleration on a centrifuge back to 1-g and the transition from positive acceleration on the flight to zero-g. I felt somewhat strange for the first few minutes. The view out of the window is a tremendous distraction as the spacecraft yaws around and the earth and the booster come into full view for the first time. We all noted a strong desire to concentrate on the tremendous view out of the window. Atlas 130D was only about 200 yards away from me. It was certainly beautiful. I could read the lettering on the sides and could see various details of the sustainer. It was a very bright silver in color, with a frosty white band around the center portion of it. It was still wisping vapor from the aft end. It was yawed [tilted] approximately 15° to 20° to its left. I had it in sight for a total of approximately 8 minutes. The front end was slowly turning in counterclockwise rotation.

Despite these distractions, the many hours of training took over and we all proceeded to do our tasks as scheduled. After a few minutes I readily adapted to the new environment and felt completely at ease. Weightlessness is extremely comfortable. After a pilot has once experienced weightlessness in space flight, he should almost immediately adapt to this condition when exposed to it again. We all even tended to forget we were weightless. . . .

Viewing the Earth from Space

During the day, the earth has a predominately bluish cast. I found that green showed up very little. Water looked very blue, and heavy forest areas looked blue-green. The only really distinctive green showed up in the high Tibetan area. Some of the high lakes were a bright emerald green and looked like those found in a copper-sulphate mining area. The browns of the Arabian desert showed up quite distinctly, but the Sahara was not quite so brown. If you are looking straight down on things, the color is truer than if you are looking at an angle.

I could detect individual houses and streets in the low-humidity and cloudless areas such as the Himalaya mountain area, the Tibetan plain, and the southwestern desert area of the U.S. I saw several individual houses with smoke coming from the chimneys in the high country around the Himalayas. The wind was apparently quite brisk and out of the south. I could see fields, roads, streams, lakes. I saw what I took to be a vehicle along a road in the Himalaya area and in the Arizona-West Texas area. I could first see the dust blowing off the road, then could see the road clearly, and when the light was right, an object that was probably a vehicle.

I saw a steam locomotive by seeing the smoke first; then I noted the object moving along what was apparently a track. This was in northern India. I also saw the wake of a boat in a large river in the Burma-India area.

At times during the day, the pattern of the sun coming through the window was hot on my suit. I could also feel heat on the inside of the window right through my glove. Like Scott, I never tired of looking at the sunsets. As the sun begins to get down towards the horizon, it is very well defined, quite difficult to look at, and not diffused as when you look at it through the atmosphere. It is a very bright white; almost the bluish white color of an arc lamp. As it begins to impinge on the horizon line, it undergoes a spreading, or flattening effect. The sky begins to get quite dark and gives the impression of deep blackness. This light spreading out from the sun is a bright orange color which moves out under a narrow band of bright blue that is always visible throughout the daylight period. As the sun sets farther, it is replaced by a bright gold-orange band which extends out for some distance on either side, defining the horizon even more clearly. The sun goes below the horizon rapidly, and the orange band still persists but gets considerably fainter as the black sky bounded by dark blue bands follows it on down. You do see a glow after the sun has set, although it is not ray-like. I could still tell exactly where the sun had set a number of seconds afterward.

At night I could see lightning. Sometimes five or six different cumulus buildups were visible at once. I could not see the lightning directly, but the whole cumulus mass of clouds would light up. From space, ground lights twinkle, whereas stars do not. I could not distinguish features on the moon. It was a partial moon at night, but it appeared full when it was setting in the daytime. It was quite bright at night, but on the day side it was a lightish blue color. . . .

Electrical Problems Arise

On the 19th orbital pass, I had been switching the warning light control switch to the "off" position in order to darken completely the interior of the spacecraft and thus become dark adapted.

When I returned the switch from the "off" to "dim" position, the 0.05g green light illuminated. I immediately turned off the ASCS 0.05g switch fuse and the emergency 0.05g fuse. Thereafter, we made three checks to verify that the ASCS 0.05g relay functions were operative. Since the amp-cal was now latched into the reentry mode, the attitude gyros were no longer operational.

The 250 v-amp main inverter failed to operate on the 21st pass. At about 33:03:00 g.e.t. the automatic changeover light for the standby inverter came on. I had noticed two small fluctuations in the ammeter just previous to this time and had gone through an electrical check; everything appeared normal. The temperature on the 250 v-amp inverter was about 115° F. The temperature on the fans inverter was about 125° F, and the standby inverter was about 95° F. At this point the light came on and I checked the inverters. The 250 v-amp inverter was still reading about 115° F on temperature, but it was indicating 140 volts on the ASCS a-c bus voltage. I then turned it off. At that time I selected the slug position (manual selection of the standby inverter for the ASCS) and found that the standby inverter would not start. I put the switch back to the "off" position of ASCS a-c power and elected to make a purely manual, or fly-by-wire, retrofire and reentry.

Analysis of these malfunctions illustrated that the entire Mercury network had developed an operational concept of teamwork that culminated in an almost perfect example of cooperation between the ground and the spacecraft on the MA-9 flight. Almost everyone followed the prestated ground rules exactly, and the radio discipline was excellent.

Reentry to Earth

All of us believed that we could control attitude manually during retrofire. However, the flight plans call for autopilot control. Nevertheless, because of failures of one type or another, Wally's was the only flight in which only the autopilot controlled attitude during retrofire. John had trouble with a low-torque thruster and elected to assist the autopilot with the manual proportional system. Scott had a problem with the horizon scanner and controlled during retrofire with the fly-by-wire and manual proportional systems. I had a malfunction associated with one of the control relays which eliminated my autopilot as well as my attitude indicators. Therefore I had to initiate retrofire, use window view for attitude reference, and control the spacecraft with the manual proportional system. This was no problem, though I did have some difficulty reading the rate indicators due to the large variation in illumination between the inside and outside of the spacecraft. . . .

As with the others, there was no doubt in my mind when the retrorockets fired. They produce a good solid thump which you can see and hear. However, our sensations at the time they fired were different. John Glenn felt like he had reversed direction and was going "back toward Hawaii." Scott Carpenter felt that he came to a standstill. Wally Schirra and I did not feel that the motion of the spacecraft changed. . . .

Landing in the Ocean

Landing at a rate of 30 fps with the landing bag down is a good solid jolt, but certainly tolerable. In fact, one does not really have to be in an ideal position and braced tightly to be able to take this momentary shock in good shape.

There have been varied opinions among the pilots of all the Mercury space flights as to the sensations encountered upon landing in water. When the spacecraft rolls over and goes under the water, there is a natural tendency to wonder if it will sink or float and whether it will right itself. One item we stressed in training was that of preparing during the descent on the parachute to evacuate the spacecraft immediately after landing in the event it starts to sink. If the pilot knows that the recovery forces are in the immediate area, this first period on the water is considerably more relaxed and enjoyable.

By the time the landing occurs, the pilot is perspiring profusely. The air from the snorkels is quite cooling, but the cabin is fairly warm and humid.

Almost the full gamut of recovery procedures were used in the course of the Mercury program. The recovery procedure is greatly simplified if the spacecraft lands near a recovery ship. In this case, the spacecraft can be lifted out of the water directly onto the deck. However, all the procedures would be simplified even more if land landings were made.

When I first stepped from the spacecraft on board the *USS Kearsarge* I felt fine. As I stood still waiting on a blood pressure check, I began to feel dizzy. I mentioned this to the doctors, who then started moving me along. As soon as I took two or three steps, I immediately began to feel clear-headed once more, and at no time did I become dizzy again.

Equal Pay for Equal Work

By Ed Townsend

Attempts to create equality for women in the workplace had been placed in front of Congress for almost two decades. Through legislation, executive orders, and judicial decisions, equal opportunity for women in employment and education became a federal goal. This goal came closer to being realized when Congress passed the Equal Pay Act of 1963, which was an amendment to the Fair Labor Standards Act, a law that attempted to remove discrimination in the types of jobs to which women could apply. The Equal Pay Act of 1963 prohibited employers and unions from paying wages based on gender. The law mandated equal pay for women in jobs that required equal skill, effort, and responsibility and which were performed under similar working conditions.

On June 10, 1963, President John F. Kennedy signed the initiative into law. On signing this landmark legislation, President Kennedy remarked, "This measure adds to our laws another structure basic to democracy. It will add protection at the working place for women, the same rights . . . that they have enjoyed at the polling place." Journalist Ed Townsend explains in this June 3, 1963, article from the *Christian Science Monitor* the initial impact on businesses, exemptions not covered by the law, and the importance of this step in achieving equality between the sexes.

Ed Townsend, "U.S. Women Reach for Equal Pay Packs," *The Christian Science Monitor*, vol. 55, June 3, 1963. Copyright © 1963 by The Christian Science Publishing Society. All rights reserved. Reproduced by permission.

After almost two decades of debate, legislation now has been enacted to require equal pay for men and women doing the same type of work for the same employer. The measure, on Mr. Kennedy's desk now, would go into effect one year after the President signs it. There are sharp disagreements over what will happen then.

Advocates of an equal-pay law say that it will be a boon to the national economy and that it will increase the earnings of women workers and stimulate business.

Critics in the business community warn that the new regulations will cause a serious squeeze on the profits of many employers and could result in a reduction of job opportunities for women.

Toward Wage Equity

Nobody has reliable figures on how many women would be affected by the new law or on how much pay costs would be raised. The final measure adopted by Senate and House is considerably modified from initial proposals. It contains more exemptions and offers plenty of leeway for differences in pay under certain conditions.

According to the AFL-CIO and other sponsors of equal-pay legislation, the measure as enacted "does not fully meet the need for effective legislation." But, they say, it is "an important first step" in a campaign that will continue.

Business foes of the proposition are well aware that the new legislation is to be regarded only as a foot in the door; they already are girding for new pressures to come. Their opposition is not to the idea that women should be paid as much as men. All else being equal, most would agree to that.

Offering Financial Relief

But, they contend, it costs more to employ women, so that if men and women are paid the same hourly wage, the employment costs for the women will be considerably higher as a result of a variety of fringe factors.

The new measure takes this into consideration—not as much as most employers would have liked it to—but still enough to relieve their total cost problems somewhat. They would be more encouraged about this if they weren't so aware that they face the uncertainty of administrative interpretations and stubborn new demands for even more equality.

There is general agreement on one thing: The new measure is much more significant than it might first appear.

Exemptions to Equal Pay

It would apply only to women already covered by the Fair Labor Standards Act—some 6,000,000 women, or roughly one-fourth of those working.

The exemptions are essentially the same as those in the Wage-Hour Law: Those not employed in interstate commerce are not covered—including many hotel and restaurant workers, laundry workers, those employed in such services as dry-cleaning establishments, many secretaries and professional or technical workers, and retail clerks whose employers are not engaged in interstate commerce.

Labor protests that too many women would be excluded.

Generally, the measure would require equal pay for work requiring the same or equal skill, effort, and responsibility performed under similar working conditions.

Wage differentials would be allowed—if at all—only for factors other than the sex of the worker. These would include the provisions of seniority systems and merit and piecework pay programs—but "other valid exceptions" may be considered on a case by case basis.

Administration and enforcement would be by the Labor Department's wage-and-hours division—critics were assured there would be "no new bureaucracy" with a new set of rules and a new corps of investigators.

Allowing for Legal Action

Employees would be able to sue for equal pay, as they now are allowed to for violations of minimum wage and overtime rules, or the Secretary of Labor may bring an action on behalf of employees—to recover the unpaid differences between rates for men and women and to enjoin their employer from further violations.

Criminal actions would be possible for willful violations.

Pay of men could not be reduced under the law: If there is a differential, the lower rate would have to be raised.

Even employers have agreed through the years that, generally, women are paid a lower wage than men. Unions and women's organizations long have attacked the differential as an unjustifiable and archaic double standard.

For 18 years, labor has campaigned to outlaw "discrimination" in pay because of sex. Bills to require equal pay for equal work were introduced in Congress in every session for years. In 1962, for the first time, real moves were made, with administration backing, for such a bill's passage. The moves failed.

Efforts were renewed this year, with even stronger support on a bipartisan basis. Extended committee hearings put the equal-pay issue into the public spotlight.

Additional Costs

Testimony by employers showed that the question of equal pay for women was by no means as simple as it would seem to be. Typically, a spokesman for Owens Illinois Glass Company said that a survey showed that its additional cost for employing women runs at least 30.1 cents an hour.

This included the cost of greater absenteeism, greater labor turnover, longer lunch and rest periods, more expensive health and welfare benefits, and special facilities required for women employees.

Employers now contend that if proper consideration isn't given to these extra labor costs in Department of Labor authorizations of "realistic" wage rates, fewer women will be employed.

Supporters of the equal-pay legislation aren't convinced. They note that many women are employed—in electrical manufacturing and electronics industries, for example—not because they can be hired for less but because they are better adapted to the work to be done.

As for the possibility that job opportunities for women may shrink, Assistant Secretary of Labor Esther Peterson said a few days ago, "We are willing to take our chances."

George Wallace's Last Stand for Segregation

By E. Culpepper Clark

George Wallace was one of America's most outspoken supporters of states' rights and of racial segregation. During the campaign to become governor of Alabama in 1962, he told audiences in regards to integration in the public school system that, "Alabama is not going to retreat one inch. I don't care what other states do. I have announced that I would draw a line in the dust. And I shall stand in the door to block the entry of federal troops or federal marshals or anyone else. They will have to arrest me before they integrate the University of Alabama." Wallace's campaign was popular with the white voters and he easily won the election. On June 11, 1963, Wallace blocked the enrollment of African American students James Hood and Vivian Malone at the University of Alabama, making him one of the country's leading figures against the civil rights movement. Martin Luther King Jr. was quoted as saying that Wallace was "perhaps the most dangerous racist in America today." Many critics also believe that his defiant stance against integration encouraged the assassination of Medgar Evers, a well-known Mississippi civil rights activist, the following day.

Although Wallace lost his battle to stop integration at the University of Alabama, he continued to resist the demands of John F. Kennedy and other officials of the federal government to integrate Alabama's education system. On September 5, 1963, he ordered schools in Bir-

E. Culpepper Clark, *The Schoolhouse Door: Segregation's Last Stand at the University of Alabama.* New York: Oxford University Press, 1993. Copyright © 1993 by E. Culpepper Clark. All rights reserved. Reproduced by permission of Oxford University Press, Inc.

mingham to close and asked reporters "What good was it doing to force these decisions when white people nowhere in the South want integration? What this country needs is a few first-class funerals, and some political funerals, too." A week later a bomb exploded outside the Sixteenth Street Baptist Church in Birmingham, Alabama, killing four schoolgirls who had been attending Sunday school classes. The following excerpt from author E. Culpepper Clark's 1993 book, *The Schoolhouse Door: Segregation's Last Stand at the University of Alabama*, reports on the standoff at the university and emphasizes the power of the federal government over the ability of an individual state in dictating national policy.

[Activist] Jeff Bennett moved into the president's mansion Monday night and slept like a baby. [Special counsel to the Justice Department, Nicholas] Katzenbach got no sleep. Vivian Malone and Jimmy Hood, who had their final meeting for last-minute details at 11 P.M., spent the evening in the home of Arthur Shores's secretary, Agnes Studemeyer, and her husband, whose hobby of making and repairing guitars drew some of the evening's attention. Malone had already put herself into a calm, almost trance-like state as she concentrated on events beyond the next day's dramatics—what her classes would be like, life on the campus, even graduation. The air of calm resignation served her well through the days ahead. More immediately, she and Hood woke to the pungent smell of Agnes Studemeyer's famous hot rolls.

Tuesday broke beautifully over the campus. The trees already wore their lush summer green, while the grass retained the tender growth of May's first warm evenings. The forecast called for unusually hot weather, but before 9 o'clock in the morning, one could still hope for a pleasant late spring day. Tommye Rose fixed breakfast for the mansion guests that included Bennett and a couple of the president's closest friends. One was Wyatt Cooper, husband of Gloria Vanderbilt and a budding writer, a friend and cousin from Rose's Mississippi youth. Several of the trustees also came for breakfast, including Caddell and McCorvey. All the trustees were to assemble at the mansion by 9 o'clock, then go to Little Hall, a short block away. Little Hall housed the physical education gymnasium and most of the athletic offices. The president and the trustees would assemble in Bear Bryant's office on the ground floor at the southwest corner of the building. The windows offered a good view of the north entrance to Foster Auditorium.

The Schoolhouse Door

The schoolhouse door was neither little nor red. Built in part with Public Works Administration funds and completed in 1939, Foster served as a multipurpose facility with a seating capacity of 5,400. Everything from graduation exercises to basketball games were held there. It was the site of President Carmichael's grave convocations during the Lucy crisis [when evidence of a missing link between man and ape was found]. University people remembered it more fondly for an event that took place a year later. With the University of North Carolina's national championship team visiting, an Alabama player took a rebound, spun, and hurled what remained until recent times the longest shot in college basketball. The building itself was stolid, 1930s' architecture, but above its north entrance rose six columns to give the otherwise drab structure a classical façade. Beneath the colonnade three doors admitted students into the gymnasium, doors that looked across the way to Farrah Hall, the university's law school. The afternoon before the confrontation, Bill Jones and Bennett directed workers to paint a semicircle in front of the center door. Behind that line, Wallace, facing the law school he had attended, would defy the federal court order.

At 8 o'clock Eastern time, 7 o'clock Alabama time, [U.S. Attorney General] Robert Kennedy left McLean for the drive into the capital. Before leaving, he called the Pentagon and learned that the [Alabama National] Guard could be federalized and deployed in less time than originally thought. (Since Guardsmen were already located just off campus, the only difficulty would come in getting General Henry V. Graham, who was on maneuvers at Fort McClellan, onto campus in time to command the units.) Kennedy arrived at the Justice Department thirty-five minutes later with three of his children in tow. [Head of Justice Department's Civil Rights Division] Burke Marshall was waiting. In Birmingham, Katzenbach and General [Creighton] Abrams prepared to escort Hood and Malone to Tuscaloosa.

Wallace Heads Toward the School

At 9:15 Central time, 10:15 Washington time, George Wallace emerged from the Stafford to a chorus of "Bless your heart; Bless your heart" and pats on the back from a cluster of women on hand to express affection and to wish him well. Before ducking into an awaiting car, [Montgomery lawyer John] Kohn approached Wallace and said, "You have Divine blessing, today, Governor. There is absolute peace here. It is a great tribute to this city and to this state—the people have shown great dignity. Good luck and may God bless you." Though overblown, Kohn's words genuinely moved Wallace toward what he considered his noble purpose. On arrival, Wallace saw 150 patrolmen in a cordon around the entrance to Foster. He waved as he approached the door where Bill Jones waited to give him last-minute instructions about the podium and the microphone. The governor wore a cool blue shirt for television. He jauntily strode the gymnasium floor joking and shaking hands with students. By 9:50 he settled himself in a comfortable air-conditioned office just inside the entrance. Ben Allen, the state investigator, was among those with him. "He was highly nervous," Allen remembered, "highly nervous, wonderin' if in fact they were gonna arrest him. Wonderin' if the federal authorities were gonna put him in jail. And I know it was awfully hot. We had men stationed on top of these buildings in this hundred-degree weather, stationed up there with rifles, and I don't see how they stood the heat." On several occasions Wallace turned to Allen and asked, "Ben, do you think they'll actually arrest me?"

(Whether Wallace was nervous, scared, or acting irrationally is important. It goes to the question of how much threat Wallace posed to the American liberal-democratic tradition. If unstable, he could be dismissed as another in a long line of gargoylish demagogues. If not, he represented something more. His enemies, and even some allies, seized upon his nervous behavior as evidence of an irrational streak. However, Ben Allen, like all the others, probably misread the governor. Wallace often used question-begging to turn the table on his enemies. Later, when an opponent blamed Wallace with indirect responsibility for JFK's assassination, the governor went around for days asking people if they thought he had helped kill the President. Put another way, the question Wallace asked Allen was: "You don't think they'll be fool enough to arrest me, do you?" Later Wallace dismissed the prospect of jail, saying "that if he were brought to trial on contempt charges, he was going to ask 250,000 Alabamians to come to his trial"—not an improbable figure. Had he wanted them in Tuscaloosa, they would have been there by the busloads. Moreover, if Wallace was nervous while waiting in the anteroom, it never showed on camera.)

The Federal Agents Head Toward the School

A phone conversation between Katzenbach and Robert Kennedy delayed the departure for the schoolhouse door by about fifteen minutes. Shortly after eight the caravan headed down U.S. 11 with Guardsmen, state troopers, and marshals making up the van. Katzenbach and [special counsel John] Doar rode with Malone and Hood. Like everybody that day, they made light talk to relieve the tension. As they rolled past the small community of Vance, about twenty miles east of Tuscaloosa, a message reached the convoy that the Attorney General wanted to speak to Katzenbach. The radio-phone hookup, however, malfunctioned. Spotting a little church up ahead, the car carrying Malone and Hood along with another carload of marshals pulled into a cemetery on a hill behind the church. Another car wheeled in to take Katzenbach to a nearby grocery store to place his call. Katzenbach was away for what seemed like an hour but actually was closer to thirty minutes. During this time the students and their escorts walked up under the shade of an old cedar tree. . . .

Of immediate concern for Katzenbach and Kennedy was difficulty in locating General Graham and what effect it might have on the day's planning. Kennedy also wanted to know once more what Katzenbach planned to say to the governor. Shortly after ten Katzenbach returned, conferred with Doar, and the caravan resumed its course, rolling into Tuscaloosa's east side around 10:20, heading toward the Army Reserve Center about a mile west of campus in the downtown area. At 10:29 Hood and Malone arrived at the Center with a four-car escort of marshals. They stayed in their car while a repairman worked on the malfunctioning radio transmitter. As they waited, Secretary of State Dean Rusk, in Washington, signed the presidential "cease and desist" proclamation, a copy of which Katzenbach would present to the governor. At 10:41 the motorcade (now three cars) left for campus. At 10:45 they passed the first barricade at Tenth Avenue and Tenth Street where they encountered no delay. Small groups lined the route, trying to see the much-publicized students. At Denny Stadium they turned left to University Boulevard and continued east just past the president's mansion, where they turned right, circling behind Little Hall. At 10:48, in roiling heat (the thermometer had already climbed passed 95 degrees), the three cars pulled up in front of Foster. From the shadows of the door, Wallace watched Katzenbach, [army Private Zachariah] Weaver, and [U.S. marshal Peyton] Norville approach. A year of pledges and promises, followed by months of planning, had come to this.

The Initial Confrontation with Wallace

Across the way, Rose and the trustees strained for a glimpse. The crush of reporters partially blocked their view, and Alex Pow climbed a radiator for a better vantage from which to call the action. At Foster, Jim Lipscomb, the cameraman for Drew Associates, desperately searched for his own perch. Finally, he took his belt and strapped one leg to the iron grating that covered a low window to Wallace's right. Leaning out he got an excellent camera angle, slightly above and to the side of the confrontation. With a copy of the President's proclamation in his coat pocket, Katzenbach strode forward, flanked by Weaver and Norville. Standing behind a shellacked-wood podium, with a mike slung around his neck, Wallace raised his left hand like a traffic cop to stop them. He said nothing. The silence caught Katzenbach off guard. All the things he had planned to say rushed in at once, canceling each other out. He decided to push past the line Jones and Bennett had drawn for newsmen, a line he believed to have been placed there for the show. The theatrical trappings positively angered him. Katzenbach had one other reason for standing close to the governor. He wanted to get out of the sun. Finally, he identified himself and said, "I have here President Kennedy's proclamation. I have come to ask you for unequivocal assurance that you or anyone under your control will not bar these students." Wallace said, "No." Then warily Katzenbach pushed the presidential proclamation toward Wallace, who received it. Wallace said nothing. Trying to recover the initiative, Katzenbach began to speak. A lack of sleep, coupled with Wallace's unnerving abruptness, caused the deputy attorney general's voice to quaver ever so slightly as he searched for the right words and the right tone to convey the administration's message.

Katzenbach folded his arms across his chest to avoid awkwardness of gesture or signs of anxiety. "I have come here," he stated more confidently, "to ask you now for unequivocal assurance that you will permit these students who, after all, merely want an education in the great University. . . ."

On hearing the editorial digression, Wallace stopped him. "Now you make your statement," he interrupted, "because we don't need your speech." Katzenbach said that he was in the process of making his statement, then repeated his demand for "an unequivocal assurance" that Wallace would do his constitutional duty and step aside. By now Katzenbach's pant legs showed sweat from the knees down. Wallace interrupted again, saying, "I have a statement to read." Wallace pulled out the statement he had prepared with the help of Kohn. He had rolled it nervously in his hands while waiting in the anteroom, so it was necessary to smooth it out on the podium before beginning. Then Wallace launched into a five-minute denunciation of the central government. After tracing his version of constitutional history and reviewing the tenets of sovereignty from a states' rights perspective, he said, "I stand before you today in place of thousands of other Alabamians whose presence would have confronted you had I been derelict and neglected to fulfill the responsibilities of my office." He declared the action of the central government (he seldom called it "federal" in official statements) to be an "unwelcomed, unwanted, unwarranted, and force-induced intrusion

George Wallace defied the federal government by attempting to prevent two black students from entering the University of Alabama.

upon the campus of the University of Alabama." He closed with a proclamation of his own: "I . . . hereby denounce and forbid this illegal and unwarranted action by the central government."

Having finished, Wallace cleared his throat, took a funny little "skip step backward" and "hopped into the doorway" as two burly patrolmen closed in beside him. Katzenbach tried once more. "I take it from the statement that you are going to stand in the door and that you are not going to carry out the orders of the court, and that you are going to resist us from doing so. Is that so?" Wallace replied flatly, "I stand according to my statement." Katzenbach started again. "I'm not interested in this show," he declared. Then turning slightly toward the cameras, "I do not know what the purpose of the show is." With mounting exasperation Katzenbach grew more confident. "It is a simple problem, scarcely worth this kind of attention. . . . From the outset, Governor, all of us have known that the final chapter of this history will be the admission of these students. . . . I ask you once again to reconsider. . . ." Wallace stared straight ahead, chin thrust forward, refusing to say anything. Katzenbach tried a fourth time only to be greeted by silence. Thus denied, Katzenbach wheeled and walked toward the waiting cars. In all, Wallace's part of the show lasted about fifteen minutes, and it was a standoff. The next move was Katzenbach's. . . .

President Kennedy Federalizes National Guard Units

The President had been meeting with congressional leaders all morning to discuss his civil rights legislation. When the call came through shortly after noon Alabama time, he was in conference with the minority leadership and gave his assent over the phone; whereupon Robert Kennedy called Cyrus Vance, Secretary of the Army. The President did not sign the authorization until after his meeting with the Republicans, 1:35 P.M. Washington time, and by then the wheels were already in motion. The administration's procedure paralleled that used by Eisenhower at Little Rock [when its public schools were desegregated]—proclamation followed by executive order. At 12:05 P.M. Alabama time, the Chief of the National Guard Bureau in the Pentagon called Adjutant General Alfred C. Harrison of the Alabama Guard directing him to report immediately to headquarters in Montgomery. There he would be designated Commanding General, Alabama Area Command. Brigadier General Henry V. Graham of the Alabama contingent of the 31st Dixie Division had been directed "to proceed to Tuscaloosa to assume command of operations in that city." The Pentagon ordered all other units to remain at their home stations or field training sites, "prepared to move on four (4) hour notice" and ordered to initiate "training in civil disturbances and riot control with particular emphasis on the use of chemical munitions and gas masks." Threats of Klan disturbances in other cities necessitated these statewide precautions.

Pitting an Alabama General Against Wallace

General Graham was inspecting troops on summer training maneuvers at Fort McClellan. He knew nothing of the role assigned him. As he helicoptered back toward the air field, he got an urgent call to contact his chief of staff, which he did on landing. Graham's aide held a phone to connect him with Colonel W.G. Johnson, the senior regular army adviser to the Alabama Guard who had the Army Operations Plan for the entire state. Colonel Johnson told Graham to report to General Abrams in Tuscaloosa immediately. Not yet appreciating the urgency, Graham said that it would be evening before he could get there. Johnson said, "General, there's a helicopter right outside your headquarters building waiting for you to take you to Tuscaloosa—now! You are to report forthwith." Graham said, "Yes sir," but still took a quick shower to remove sweat and dust from the morning's inspection. Within minutes he lifted off for Tuscaloosa, 120 miles by road but less than an hour by air. With him was army Colonel Gene Cook, the only officer at Fort McClellan who knew the plan. . . .

At 1:40 P.M., Graham's helicopter set down on an apron adjacent to Fort Brandon Armory. He proceeded immediately to the Army Reserve Center where General Abrams briefed him on the morning's developments and gave him instructions for confronting the governor that afternoon. Graham did not welcome the idea of forcefully removing the governor from the door. If it came to that, his business career almost certainly would be ruined. Nonetheless he understood his duty. Fortunately a call came through from General Taylor Hardin, a close friend of the governor's and later his finance director. Hardin wanted to come to the Reserve Center and speak with General Graham privately.

The two men met in a small conference room. Hardin told Graham that Wallace would step aside peaceably if allowed to make a statement. While Hardin waited, Graham conveyed the message to General Abrams, who in turn consulted with Katzenbach. Though reluctant to give Wallace another platform, the deal was cut. So at approximately 2:30 on the afternoon of the 11th, the Justice Department at last received what it had sought for two weeks: a direct assurance from Wallace that he would go without being forcibly removed or arrested. Earlier in the day Wallace's press secretary told reporters that the governor had "never said he will oppose the armed might of the federal government," and another aide, following the morning standoff, said, "The governor is waiting for the troops. There will be no shoving or pushing. There may be a minute's word battle and then he will fly back to Montgomery or to Huntsville if necessary." These were comforting words, and in line with what the Justice Department had heard since Jeff Bennett's call to Burke Marshall on March 19, but indirect assurances were no substitute in Katzenbach's mind for the kind of confirmation provided by Hardin. . . .

General Graham Removes Wallace

Sizing up the situation at Foster, General Graham sent 100 Guardsmen to the campus. At 3:16 three troop carriers escorted by motorcycle police roared up to the side and rear of Foster. Infantrymen, in green fatigues and carrying M-1 rifles, formed a line up the west side of the auditorium. Another convoy arrived in front of Denny Chimes, across from the president's mansion on University Boulevard. General Graham arrived in a green, unmarked command car. He decided to march a platoon (35 men) to the auditorium, a Special Forces unit under Colonel Henry Cobb, a classmate of Katzenbach's at Princeton. Graham spotted [Alabama National Guard Colonel Albert J.] Lingo and the two saluted and conferred briefly before Graham decided that "the platoon in steel helmets and weapons was an overkill," and left the unit between Farrah and Little Halls near University Boulevard. With four sergeants in green berets, he donned his soft cap and moved toward the final confrontation. On the way he huddled with Katzenbach, Norville, and Weaver, who fell in behind the General with the four sergeants bringing up the rear. They strode purposefully toward the wall of state troopers and reporters. The silence was eerie, disturbed only by the soft whirring of cameras and popping flashbulbs. Seeing their approach, Seymore Trammell turned toward the entrance and clapped on his straw hat as a signal for Wallace to take his stand. At 3:30, General Graham, in combat fatigues with the Confederate battle flag of the 31st Dixie Division stitched to his breast pocket, came forward and saluted the governor. Snappily Wallace returned the salute. Graham then said, "It is my sad duty to ask you to step aside, on order of the President of the United States." The words were heartfelt. Earlier General Abrams offered to have a Justice Department staffer write a statement for Graham, but the General said it would not be necessary. The simplicity of his words expressed the sentiments of a majority of the state's moderate whites.

Wallace said, "General, I want to make a statement." Graham replied, "Certainly, sir," then stepped to one side. Speaking from notes scribbled on a spiral calendar pad, Wallace declared, "But for the unwarranted federalization of the Alabama National Guard, I would, at this moment, be your Commander-in-Chief—in fact I am your Commander-in-Chief, and as Governor of this state, I know this is a bitter pill for members of the Alabama National Guard to swallow." Wallace asked that all Alabama citizens remain "calm and restrained." Declaring the National Guard "our brothers," Wallace said, "Alabama is winning this fight against Federal interference because we are awakening the people to the trend toward military dictatorship in this country. I am returning to Montgomery to continue working for constitutional government to benefit all Alabamians—black and white." With that, Wallace and his entourage walked quickly toward waiting patrol cars. The clock showed 3:33 P.M. As the governor's motorcade pulled away, Wallace kept repeating a warm "Come back to see us in Alabama" to a bank of reporters demanding to know whether there would be a press conference. When the motorcade turned onto University Boulevard, students and university staff who had been kept away from the scene showed their approval by applauding the governor. High atop Foster Auditorium, one of the four patrolmen stationed there waved a white flag.

A Peaceful Outcome Is Reached

In Bear Bryant's office the trustees congratulated themselves on a peaceful outcome to a ten-year ordeal. A few of the older men shed tears as they saw their beloved institution pass into the new era, but the general feeling was one of relief. Rose and his staff

could be satisfied with the elaborate planning that helped make
the schoolhouse door the most publicized nonviolent confrontation of the civil rights movement. Even if it was not in any real
sense the university's show, it had been staged on the campus and
most of the nation came away with the feeling that Alabama's
university and its president contrasted favorably with the state's
government and its governor.

In Washington Robert Kennedy stood with his staff, arms
folded, listening to the drama over radio. He had his coat on now,
ready to go to the White House. His expression did not change
as the announcer reported that Wallace was leaving the door, but
when the commentator relayed Wallace's claim that he was winning the constitutional fight, a grin of disbelief flickered across
the Attorney General's face. Kennedy turned to Bob Shuker of
Drew Associates and said that the film crew should abandon its
plan to shoot at Hickory Hill that evening and instead go to the
White House. He provided a driver and car. The speech was on.
Meanwhile, Jim Lipscomb took his transistorized camera and
rode with Wallace to the Tuscaloosa airport. Wallace continued
to look mean-spirited as he stammered that some politicians were
going to pay at the polls come next year, that the presidency
could not be won without the South.

With Wallace's departure, Jimmy Hood and Vivian Malone
entered the schoolhouse door to a spattering of applause. From
an upper-floor window a student unfurled an American flag.
Registration took less than fifteen minutes but looked almost sur-
real on the near-empty gym floor. A full cadre of faculty and staff
served the two students who had completed most preliminaries
earlier. Both had had a chance to change clothes and freshen up
between the first and second confrontation. Hood went in first,
as always nattily dressed with his snap-brim hat and briefcase.
Malone followed, wearing a two-piece pink outfit and, in the
style of the early sixties, a short bouffant hair-do with bangs. She
looked serious until a reporter drawled, "How do you feel,
ma'am?" She answered with a smile. Hood and Malone stayed
in the dorms that night, where student leaders had been assigned
to make them welcome. Officials worried over a bomb threat
against Mary Burke Hall, but a search turned up nothing. That
night General Graham slept on a sofa in the lobby. Upstairs, Vivian Malone collected her thoughts alone in her single room. Upstairs, also, slept the general's daughter.

Address to the Nation on Civil Rights

By John F. Kennedy

Several events in 1963 would push the Kennedy administration toward the development of a civil rights bill, but the increase in violence used against civil rights activists created a sense of urgency that had not yet existed in prior presidencies. Segregationists were often making violent stands against marchers and activists working in voter registration drives. Militant blacks were preaching policies of violent reaction and encouraging blacks to take by force what the government refused to give them under the law. The convergence of these factors compelled President John F. Kennedy to push forward a civil rights bill. His major concern was his ability to gather support from southern moderates. President Kennedy desired to draft legislation that would have a significant impact on the plight of African Americans, but without the support of southern senators, any civil rights legislation would represent only a token change and do nothing significant toward the goal of securing equality.

From the onset of 1963, several other key events also occurred to increase public support for a civil rights bill. Alabama, the beacon of segregation in the South, elected George Wallace as governor. In his inaugural speech, Wallace declared "Segregation now! Segregation tomorrow! Segregation forever!" Wallace's speech served as the battle cry of white southern resistance. Civil rights workers in the southern

John F. Kennedy, radio and television address to the American people, June 11, 1963.

cities of Mobile, Birmingham, and Selma were repeatedly attacked by police with police dogs and fire hoses. The American public witnessed these events on television and became increasingly outraged at these horrific acts of violence. In the wake of these events and with growing national support, President John F. Kennedy appealed to Congress to draft civil rights legislation. President Kennedy delivered this speech to the American people on June 11, 1963, and called on Congress to put an end to segregation by affording blacks equality under the law.

T his afternoon, following a series of threats and defiant statements, the presence of Alabama National Guardsmen was required on the University of Alabama to carry out the final and unequivocal order of the United States District Court of the Northern District of Alabama. That order called for the admission of two clearly qualified young Alabama residents who happened to have been born Negro.

That they were admitted peacefully on the campus is due in good measure to the conduct of the students of the University of Alabama, who met their responsibilities in a constructive way.

I hope that every American, regardless of where he lives, will stop and examine his conscience about this and other related incidents. This Nation was founded by men of many nations and backgrounds. It was founded on the principle that all men are created equal, and that the rights of every man are diminished when the rights of one man are threatened.

Protecting the Rights of the Free

Today we are committed to a worldwide struggle to promote and protect the rights of all who wish to be free. And when Americans are sent to Viet-Nam or West Berlin, we do not ask for whites only. It ought to be possible, therefore, for American students of any color to attend any public institution they select without having to be backed up by troops.

It ought to be possible for American consumers of any color to receive equal service in places of public accommodation, such as hotels and restaurants and theaters and retail stores, without being forced to resort to demonstrations in the street, and it ought to be possible for American citizens of any color to register and to vote in a free election without interference or fear of reprisal.

It ought to be possible, in short, for every American to enjoy the privileges of being American without regard to his race or his color. In short, every American ought to have the right to be treated as he would wish to be treated, as one would wish his children to be treated. But this is not the case.

The Current Negro Disadvantage

The Negro baby born in America today, regardless of the section of the Nation in which he is born, has about one-half as much chance of completing a high school as a white baby born in the same place on the same day, one-third as much chance of completing college, one-third as much chance of becoming a professional man, twice as much chance of becoming unemployed, about one-seventh as much chance of earning $10,000 a year, a life expectancy which is 7 years shorter, and the prospects of earning only half as much.

This is not a sectional issue. Difficulties over segregation and discrimination exist in every city, in every State of the Union, producing in many cities a rising tide of discontent that threatens the public safety. Nor is this a partisan issue. In a time of domestic crisis men of good will and generosity should be able to unite regardless of party or politics. This is not even a legal or legislative issue alone. It is better to settle these matters in the courts than on the streets, and new laws are needed at every level, but law alone cannot make men see right.

We are confronted primarily with a moral issue. It is as old as the scriptures and is as clear as the American Constitution.

Raising the Question of Equality

The heart of the question is whether all Americans are to be afforded equal rights and equal opportunities, whether we are going to treat our fellow Americans as we want to be treated. If an American, because his skin is dark, cannot eat lunch in a restaurant open to the public, if he cannot send his children to the best public school available, if he cannot vote for the public officials who represent him, if, in short, he cannot enjoy the full and free life which all of us want, then who among us would be content to have the color of his skin changed and stand in his place? Who among us would then be content with the counsels of patience and delay?

One hundred years of delay have passed since President Lincoln freed the slaves, yet their heirs, their grandsons, are not fully free. They are not yet freed from the bonds of injustice. They are not yet freed from social and economic oppression. And this Nation, for all its hopes and all its boasts, will not be fully free until all its citizens are free.

We preach freedom around the world, and we mean it, and we cherish our freedom here at home, but are we to say to the world, and much more importantly, to each other that this is a land of the free except for the Negroes; that we have no second-class citizens except Negroes; that we have no class or caste system, no ghettoes, no master race except with respect to Negroes? . . .

We face, therefore, a moral crisis as a country and as a people. It cannot be met by repressive police action. It cannot be left to increased demonstrations in the streets. It cannot be quieted by token moves or talk. It is a time to act in the Congress, in your State and local legislative body and, above all, in all of our daily lives.

It is not enough to pin the blame on others, to say this is a problem of one section of the country or another, or deplore the fact that we face. A great change is at hand, and our task, our obligation, is to make that revolution, that change, peaceful and constructive for all.

Those who do nothing are inviting shame as well as violence. Those who act boldly are recognizing right as well as reality.

The Federal Government's Commitment

Next week I shall ask the Congress of the United States to act, to make a commitment it has not fully made in this century to the proposition that race has no place in American life or law. The Federal judiciary has upheld that proposition in a series of forthright cases. The executive branch has adopted that proposition in the conduct of its affairs, including the employment of Federal personnel, the use of Federal facilities, and the sale of federally financed housing.

But there are other necessary measures which only the Congress can provide, and they must be provided at this session. The old code of equity law under which we live commands for every wrong a remedy, but in too many communities, in too many parts of the country, wrongs are inflicted on Negro citizens and there are no remedies at law. Unless the Congress acts, their only remedy is in the street.

I am, therefore, asking the Congress to enact legislation giving all Americans the right to be served in facilities which are open to the public—hotels, restaurants, theaters, retail stores, and similar establishments.

This seems to me to be an elementary right. Its denial is an arbitrary indignity that no American in 1963 should have to endure, but many do. . . .

Maintaining National Solidarity

This is one country. It has become one country because all of us and all the people who came here had an equal chance to develop their talents.

We cannot say to 10 percent of the population that you can't have that right; that your children can't have the chance to develop whatever talents they have; that the only way that they are going to get their rights is to go into the streets and demonstrate. I think we owe them and we owe ourselves a better country than that.

Therefore, I am asking for your help in making it easier for us to move ahead and to provide the kind of equality of treatment which we would want ourselves; to give a chance for every child to be educated to the limit of his talents.

As I have said before, not every child has an equal talent or an equal ability or an equal motivation, but they should have the equal right to develop their talent and their ability and their motivation, to make something of themselves.

We have a right to expect that the Negro community will be responsible, will uphold the law, but they have a right to expect that the law will be fair, that the Constitution will be color blind, as Justice Harlan said at the turn of the century.

This is what we are talking about and this is a matter which concerns this country and what it stands for, and in meeting it I ask the support of all our citizens.

The Murder of Civil Rights Leader Medgar Evers

By Adam Nossiter

Medgar Evers received his B.A. degree from Alcorn University in 1954 and moved with his wife, Myrlie, to Mound Bayou, Mississippi, to perform work for the National Association for the Advancement of Colored People (NAACP). Throughout the late 1950s, Evers worked to establish local chapters of the NAACP in the area and organized boycotts of gasoline stations that refused to allow blacks to use their rest rooms.

Medgar Evers's initial work in civil rights began in 1954, shortly following the Supreme Court decision in *Brown v. the Board of Education*, which ruled segregation in publicly funded schools unconstitutional. Evers used this ruling as a legal basis for making an application to the University of Mississippi Law School. He was denied admission on the basis of racial discrimination despite the high court's ruling. Evers conducted several protest demonstrations in an unsuccessful attempt to integrate the university. His efforts gained him some national media coverage and attracted the attention of the NAACP's national office in New York. For his efforts, he was appointed Mississippi's first field secretary for the NAACP.

Evers and his wife moved to Jackson, Mississippi, where they worked together to set up a local chapter of the NAACP. While in Jackson, he began investigating violent crimes committed against blacks and sought ways to prevent further violence. His boycott of Jackson merchants in the early 1960s attracted national media attention, and his participation in the efforts to have James Meredith admitted to the University of Mississippi in 1962 brought much-needed federal assistance to the cause of integration. Evers also spearheaded many voter registration drives in an attempt to increase the amount of Negro voters in Mississippi. Evers's involvement in this and other activities increased the hatred many people felt toward Evers and other civil rights activists working in the Deep South.

On June 12, 1963, Medgar Evers was killed by an assassin's bullet as he stood in his driveway. The assassination occurred just a day after President John F. Kennedy delivered his speech on the need for Congress to pass the civil rights act, a speech that was given in response to Alabama governor George Wallace's June 11, 1963, attempt to block the integration of the University of Alabama in Tuscaloosa. The following excerpt, from author Adam Nossiter's 1994 book *Of Long Memory: Mississippi and the Murder of Medgar Evers*, discusses the last few days of Evers's life. Ironically, Evers's murder forced the end of a filibuster that had previously postponed the drafting and passage of a civil rights bill in the U.S. Senate. The civil rights bill passed in 1964 as the Civil Rights Act and was followed a year later by the Voting Rights Act of 1965.

That last month of his life was unlike any other Evers had lived through. Up until then Jackson [Mississippi] had been dead, barely on the civil rights map, its small black middle class cowed and complacent. "Lots of fear, lots of apathy," Evers told [sociologist John] Salter in the summer of 1962. A months-old boycott of downtown stores, pushed by the impetuous twenty-nine-year-old Salter, was only modestly effective and had been largely ignored by the officials in New York. Imbued with an instinctive allegiance to the growing movement for racial justice, Salter—an Arizonan, an ex-Wobbly [union activist], and part American Indian—had a high sense of romance and adventure. Two years before, he had come to the state expecting and half wanting trouble. He taught sociology at Tougaloo and headed a small NAACP youth group in the city, but the hierarchy did not take his efforts very seriously.

Suddenly, after Martin Luther King, Jr.'s triumph in Birmingham and rumors that Jackson might be next on the SCLC [Southern Christian Leadership Conference] agenda, everything changed. The downtown boycott became interesting to New York; Salter, the prime mover, was told by phone April 9 that [NAACP worker Roy] Wilkins was "extremely interested" in what was happening in Jackson. But decades of caution had made the NAACP incapable of committing itself wholesale to protest in the streets. From then until Evers's assassination, Salter rode a roller coaster of hope and despair, alternately cursing the national NAACP office when it repeatedly backed off plans for demonstrations (as it did May 10, again two weeks later, according to Salter, and finally just before Evers's death) and jubilant when it agreed to move forward, as it did at various points in between.

Challenging Segregation in Jackson

Evers rode a personal roller coaster. From the reporters who began to descend on the city, and from Salter's memoir, emerge snapshots of him in that last month urging the growing crowd forward into the streets and watching disgustedly as the crowd members are herded into paddy wagons and the makeshift barbed-wire stockade at the Jackson Fairgrounds. And he collaborated on Salter's demand to state officials May 12 [1963], for an end to segregation in parks, playgrounds, libraries, and downtown stores and restaurants.

The segregationists' response was a paternalist daydream: "We have some of the best facilities you can find anywhere," the mayor of Jackson, a Citizens' Council enthusiast named Allan Thompson, declaimed in a television speech. "Beautiful, wonderful schools, parks, playgrounds, libraries, and so many, many other things. Next, there are no slums. Have you ever thought about it?" Evers's reply came in an unprecedented appearance on a local television station May 20, secured with the help of the Federal Communications Commission. Never before had a Mississippi black man been allowed this kind of response to the segregationists.

He shot the mayor's fantasy full of holes. For seventeen minutes, to viewers all over the state, Evers gave a summation of his outlook, one rooted in the concrete and the real. Where Martin Luther King, Jr. might have traded in abstractions about racial harmony and justice, Evers drew directly on his experience: the black man, looking about Mayor Thompson's urban idyll, "sees a city," Evers said, "where Negro citizens are refused admittance to the City Auditorium and the Coliseum; his children refused a ticket to a good movie in a downtown theater; his wife and children refused service at a lunch counter in a downtown store where they trade." He was acutely aware a historic turning point had been reached: "Whether Jackson and the state choose change or not, the years of change are upon us. In the racial picture things will never be as they once were."

As a picture of truth, this was more than some Jackson whites could take. . . . Several callers to the television station went beyond registering shock at this apparition: they made a point of furiously denying the veracity of Evers's claims. "I'd just like to call in and tell you I think that's very horrible, this nigra on TV with all his lies that seem to be coming in," one man said. "Well, I won't . . . just don't even quote me. But this is the most ignorant display of ignorance I've ever heard in my life," a woman said.

A Continuing Affront to Jim Crow

He had touched the most sensitive nerve. What made it all the more dangerous for him was that he did not then retreat. On May 28 he told the crowd at the Pearl Street A.M.E. [African Methodist Episcopal] Church that the day's bloody sit-in at the downtown Woolworth's was only the beginning, and he called for a "massive offensive against segregation." The next day he angrily denounced Jackson's mayor for "talking out of two sides of his mouth and duping people" after the mayor reneged on an agreement to desegregate public facilities. On June 1, he and Roy Wilkins were arrested in a symbolic demonstration on Capitol Street. And Evers arrived at his office at seven o'clock every morning and rushed all over the city to arrange bail bond for jailed students, attended mass meetings, and met with reporters.

But he entered this whirlwind with some ambivalence: he was an NAACP man, and that organization never overcame its fear of crowd action. In his wife's memoir, he was "neither approving or disapproving" of the pivotal Woolworth sit-in. A few days before, he had exploded in anger at Salter's skepticism about the national NAACP, and he urged caution among black youths who wanted to demonstrate. His wife remembers that he "had his doubts" about demonstrations, although she says he was later "won over completely" by the students.

Support in Jackson Falters

The young people who worked with Evers feel sure about where his true allegiance lay. "He was a direct action person, in terms of where his heart was," remembers Steve Rutledge, a white Tougaloo student who worked with Salter. It was a leaning that Rutledge and his cohorts thought brought Evers directly into conflict with the conservative officials in New York.

By the middle of June's first week, reporters were beginning to pull out of Jackson because of the palpable lessening of civil rights activity. "Press releases and news conferences replaced mass marches today," a dispatch datelined June 3 began. Local organizers like Salter thought the national office was rolling back the campaign of demonstrations in Jackson. Just after his own arrest, Wilkins called for a halt to the demonstrations. He quickly relented after protests, but to Salter the message was clear. "The feeling we had was so obvious," remembers Rutledge. "They're not supporting us any more. The national officers came down and laid the law down, limiting the demonstrations."

Evers's Decline

There is a strange convergence between the way people remember Evers at the end of his life, and his demise itself. Invariably in these accounts he is worn out, exhausted, at a breaking point emotionally and physically. He was even considering a break with the NAACP, according to Salter and Ed King.

"He had aged ten years in the past two months," [Evers's wife] Myrlie wrote. "Tired" is how Salter repeatedly describes the Medgar of the final week. At home, at the sound of passing cars, he would jump out of bed and grab one of his many rifles in one motion. Police cars followed him constantly. On the last afternoon of his life, Monday, June 11, he telephoned the FBI office in New Orleans and told the agents that three days before, a police car had tried to run him down as he was crossing Franklin Street. He had had to scramble back onto the sidewalk, at which the officers had laughed. A few hours later, shortly before attending that night's meeting, Salter saw Evers standing in the nearly empty auditorium of the Masonic Temple on Lynch Street. "He was very tired and worn, with sharper lines in his face than before, and he seemed quietly sad."

In such remembrances it is as if the living, breathing Evers is being wound down by the people who knew him. An Evers stripped of vigor is an Evers with no further historical role in the present—an ironic fate for someone who saw himself as a man of action above all else. At least in people's memories, the transformation from activist to martyr-symbol had begun even before his death. To be sure, such memories must be, at least in part, a device to give comfort to people who were attached to Evers; these acquaintances are unconsciously making his murder a logical culmination for his life. But the perceived transformation is also a reflection of a sad reality: the end of his usefulness to the civil rights movement had preceded his death.

A Shot in the Dark

The evening of Tuesday, June 11, was warm and dry in Jackson. Myrlie was watching President Kennedy's unplanned, breakthrough civil rights speech, engendered in the heat of that day's showdown at the University of Alabama between Gov. George Wallace and the government, demonstrations and beatings in Virginia, and the ongoing crisis in Jackson. "We are confronted primarily with a moral issue," Kennedy had said. "It is as old as the Scriptures and as clear as the American Constitution." The words made Myrlie glad. Medgar, of course, was away at a rally, struggling to prop up the faltering Jackson civil rights campaign. The three Evers children had been allowed to wait up for him; their only chances to see him came late at night. Myrlie, reclining on the bed, drifted off, and the children argued over which program to switch to.

At midnight, Myrlie heard the sound of tires in the driveway. Medgar was home. The car door slammed closed. Then, a much louder sound, so loud in the hot, quiet night that people all over the neighborhood heard it. The children hit the floor, as they had been trained to do.

Myrlie knew what the sound was. She knew what it meant. She rushed to the door and turned on the light. He was lying there, face down. She saw the keys in his hand, and she saw the trail of blood behind him. He had managed to drag himself thirty-nine feet. The sweatshirts he had been carrying, inscribed "Jim Crow Must Go," were scattered all over the driveway. Myrlie screamed, but he did not move. The children were around him, screaming, "Please, Daddy, please get up!" Still he did not move. He had been hit with tremendous force by the bullet from a high-powered gun.

Later, the police would be struck by the large amount of blood on the driveway and the flesh spattered on the car. "It looked like somebody had butchered a hog at that point," Detective John Chamblee observed later. The bullet had struck Evers in the back, exited through his chest, crashed through his living room window, gone through another wall into the kitchen, ricocheted off the refrigerator, shattered a glass coffee pot on the sink, and landed on a cabinet. By the time detectives recovered it, this bullet was badly battered. But of one thing they were certain: it could only have been fired from a .30/06 Enfield rifle.

Up the street Betty Coley had heard a "crunching sound," then the unmistakeable noise of someone running. Kenneth Adcock had heard leaves and branches crackling: someone running, fast.

Evers had been wearing a white shirt, an easy target for the sniper. Neighbors and police lifted the dying man onto a mattress and loaded him into a station wagon. "Sit me up," Evers said. "Turn me loose." Those were his last words.

The Aftermath

In the riot that followed Evers's funeral, three days after his murder, four hundred young blacks hurled bricks, bottles, and insults at the Jackson police. "Shoot us, shoot us," the blacks cried. "No one shot them," a still surprised Hodding Carter wrote a week later. "This was not the Mississippi of five years ago," he continued. "But in the wake of Medgar Evers' death, Jackson and the state of Mississippi are not what they have been in many respects."

Carter was both prescient and right to hedge his assertion. Evers had been up against much more than just a lone racist hiding in a thicket. It became, in fact, unquestioned dogma in the Mississippi civil rights movement that the surrounding society had pulled the trigger of the .30/06 Enfield rifle. "The issue before the court was not the guilt or innocence of Delay [his nickname] Beckwith," Ed King wrote not long after Beckwith's trials in 1964, "but whether Medgar Evers was guilty enough in his agitation to deserve the death sentence which Beckwith, for all white Mississippi, had carried out."

There is no evidence to suggest a conspiracy. But what is certain is that Evers and the other civil rights workers were up against a uniquely formidable force: the structures that made up the white supremacist state.

Supporting a Nuclear Test Ban Treaty

By Richard S. Preston

Arms control advocates had campaigned for the adoption of a treaty banning all nuclear explosions since the early 1950s, when public concern was aroused as a result of radioactive fallout from atmospheric nuclear tests and the escalating arms race. Picking up on President Dwight D. Eisenhower's earlier efforts to reach agreement on a comprehensive test ban, President John F. Kennedy advanced two new draft treaty texts in August 1962. One draft outlined a comprehensive ban that included earlier American proposals for on-site inspections. A second draft proposed a limited (atmospheric) test ban. The Soviet Union rejected both draft treaties on the grounds that on-site inspections were not necessary given other advances in verification and that a partial ban would still "legalize" underground testing and allow further nuclear weapons development. Little progress was made in follow-up discussions.

On July 15, 1963, U.S., British, and Soviet negotiators met in Moscow to try to negotiate an agreement on a comprehensive nuclear test ban. Due to disagreements concerning on-site inspections, agreement on a comprehensive test ban was never reached. Negotiators turned their attention to the conclusion of a limited ban, prohibiting tests in the atmosphere, outer space, and beneath the surface of the

Richard S. Preston, "The Nuclear Test Ban Treaty," *Current History*, vol. 46, June 1964, pp. 341–45.

seas. On July 25, the Limited Test Ban Treaty was signed by all three parties. In the following article from June 1964, Richard S. Preston, a physicist at the Argonne National Laboratory, discusses the major events leading up to the passage of the Limited Test Ban Treaty as well as arguments of the era used by opponents of such a ban. The test ban treaty was ratified by the House of Representatives in August 1963, and then ratified by the Senate in October 1963, officially endorsing American support for the treaty.

The nuclear test ban treaty is widely considered to be the most significant accomplishment of 18 cold war years of negotiation on weapons control, and one of the most significant international agreements since World War II. The treaty is very popular. Worldwide sentiment in favor of it had been growing for nine years. In addition to the three original signatories over 100 nations acceded to it almost immediately. The United States Senate ratified it by a vote of 80 to 19, and public opinion polls showed overwhelming support for it.

This enthusiasm for a test ban reflects a widespread yearning to make nuclear war less likely and less devastating, and to put an end to radioactive fallout from nuclear testing. The treaty itself does little to satisfy this yearning. It is not a disarmament treaty, and it puts no restrictions on the arms race except for the prohibition of test explosions too large to be confined underground. It does not settle any outstanding issue of the cold war. Furthermore, France and China are not bound by the treaty; if nothing else prevents them, they certainly are quite likely to retrace the whole process by which the United States, Great Britain, and Russia perfected multi-megaton weapons, thereby exposing the world to a whole new generation of fallout.

Nevertheless, the signing of a test ban treaty may prove to have been a turning point in international relations. In assessing the significance of the test ban and trying to see what consequences may arise from it, it will be useful to review the development of the concept of the test ban.

Building Toward a Test Ban

The single bomb that was dropped on Hiroshima in 1945 released 1000 times as much energy as the largest of the conventional bombs of World War II. The significance of this new dimension of military destructive capability soon became widely understood. For a number of years, the major powers debated in the United Nations about techniques for limiting or eliminating nuclear weaponry. Eventually a wide range of proposals for arms limitation came under discussion, and since the early 1950's both arms reduction and complete disarmament have been subjects of East-West negotiation. . . .

Early in the negotiations, a basic pattern of disagreement on the principles of weapons control emerged. It became clear that the United States would always insist on inspection to verify that the terms of an agreement were being carried out. The United States was afraid to undertake any mutual arms reduction without assurance at every step that the other side was also complying. The Soviet Union, on the other hand, would always view inspection as a threat to the secrecy it considers indispensable for military security. Arguing that inspection would provide opportunities for outsiders to spy, the U.S.S.R. would permit inspection only at a late stage in general disarmament. . . .

Four Arguments Against U.S. Participation

The chief points of argument against United States participation in a test ban treaty are four. First, a test ban by itself would be worthless since it would have no effect on the production, stockpiling or eventual use of existing types of nuclear weapons.

Second, it would be foolhardy to trust Russia not to cheat if it could. Detection of all tests down to arbitrarily small sizes is obviously impossible, regardless of the monitoring system used. Concealed tests of small devices could lead to technical advances that would tilt the military balance in Russia's favor. The United States cannot afford to take this risk.

Third, the only safe position for the United States is one of military superiority. Continued strength requires continued efforts to improve our own nuclear capability by developing, testing, and deploying any kind of weapon, large or small, offensive or defensive, that might be militarily useful. We must continue testing.

Fourth, the fallout problem has been overemphasized. The harmful effects of global fallout are not large enough to be observable statistically in whole populations, to say nothing of the impossibility of identifying these effects in particular individuals. Fallout is one of the minor hazards we live with. The harm it does is a small price to pay for security.

That there must have been similar misgivings in Russia may be judged from the fact that the U.S.S.R. broke an early, self-imposed unilateral moratorium on tests just as serious test ban negotiations were about to start. The U.S.S.R. was also the first to break the spell of the famous long moratorium and resume tests in 1961.

Proponents of the test ban rejected the notion that continued safety could be gained by either side in a nuclear arms race. First, the concept of nuclear superiority is becoming progressively less and less meaningful militarily; by conventional standards an all-out nuclear war between strong nuclear powers would be catastrophic for both sides, even if they were not very evenly matched. . . .

Second, while we may hope that the arms race will turn into a permanent stalemate in which neither side will dare use its nuclear weapons, such a stalemate would be undependable. The frightful possibility would remain that existing nuclear arsenals could be brought into use, either suddenly as a result of miscalculation, accident, desperation, or madness, or more slowly by escalation from a conventional war.

Third, the only permanent solution to the problem is the elimination of all nuclear weapons. It may be that this can only be accomplished by total disarmament, or it may be that it cannot be accomplished at all. Nevertheless we must explore every possible approach to this goal including preliminary steps such as workable agreements on arms limitation, arms reduction, and other arms control measures.

Fourth, one possible first step is an agreement to ban nuclear tests. It is not a large step. It would stop neither the production of existing weapons nor the development of new uses and new means of delivery for them. It would cause very little disturbance of present military trends, unfortunately, but it would cause no sudden shift in the strategic balance, either. Therefore it is a first step with a good chance of being agreed upon.

Fifth, in assessing the risks inherent in this or any similar step we must keep in mind the staggering risks involved in a continuation of the nuclear arms race.

Providing Reasons for a Test Ban

Although proponents of a test ban conceded that its direct effect on the arms race would be small, they advanced other reasons for concentrating on getting a test ban treaty:

1) It would put a stop to the development of ever more frightful weapons of mass destruction.

2) The nuclear powers have thus far refrained from nuclear warfare, but the peace is unstable. The instability will be larger when there are a larger number of nuclear powers involved. Therefore it is important to prevent the spread of nuclear weapons to nations that do not yet have them. . . .

3) The arms race is a reaction to mistrust and suspicion, much of it justified. But the arms buildup aggravates the mistrust and suspicion, which in turn accelerates the arms race even faster. A test ban could help break this vicious circle both because of its small direct decelerating effect on the arms buildup, and because a demonstration by each side that it is making a genuine effort to reverse the trend should help to reduce the mistrust and suspicion.

4) Workable international control and inspection procedures would have to be developed for a test ban. If and when more comprehensive arms control measures are agreed on, it will be useful to have the valuable experience and precedent of the test ban control system to draw upon.

5) A test ban would cut off the source of fallout. Although there are only a few known cases of injury to humans that can be traced directly to fallout from testing, there is wide agreement among competent authorities that fallout is harmful. This might be considered a reasonable price to pay for military security except for two considerations. It is questionable whether this sacrifice can buy real security. And, since fallout is worldwide, it affects whole populations which have no choice in the matter. This has been a continuing cause of international bad feeling, and it would be well to eliminate it.

The March on Washington

By Henry Gemmill

In 1942 respected civil rights activist leader A. Philip Randolph first envisioned a great march on the nation's capital in order to force the federal government to change laws that established segregation. Politically, the civil rights movement at that time was neither large enough nor ready for such a mass demonstration. By the late 1950s, however, a young minister named Martin Luther King Jr. coordinated several civil rights activities that slowly changed the face of segregated cities like Birmingham and Selma, Alabama. King started working with Randolph, and in 1963, both men began to coordinate the dreamed-of March on Washington, an effort that would involve thousands of black and white civil rights activists. Buses (called Freedom Buses) and trains were organized by student activist groups and churches to transport people to Washington. In all, more than thirty chartered trains and over two thousand buses would be utilized to bring the marchers to the nation's capital. By these means, along with private transportation, more than 250,000 people gathered in Washington, D.C., on August 28, 1963.

A. Philip Randolph gave the first speech of the day. He stipulated seven goals that were demanded by the marchers. These goals included the passage of meaningful civil rights legislation, an immediate end to all school segregation, protection for all civil rights protesters against police brutality, a major public works program for all unemployed, a

Henry Gemmill, "Civil Rights March on Washington Orderly; Leaders Urge Diverse Courses of Action," *The Wall Street Journal*, vol. CLXII, August 29, 1963. Copyright © 1963 by Dow Jones & Company, Inc. All rights reserved. Reproduced by permission.

federal law prohibiting racial discrimination in the workplace, a $2 minimum wage, and self-government for the District of Columbia.

As the speeches continued, the massive amount of people pushed forward to listen. City officials became fearful of violence, although none broke out. The speeches encouraged the black people present to increase their participation in civil rights protests and activities. In this August 29, 1963, article, Henry Gemmill, staff reporter for the *Wall Street Journal*, gives a brief outline of the day's events, including the plans made by city officials to accommodate such a large throng of people.

An integrated Sunday school outing, on a mammoth scale. That's what the "March on Washington" seemed to be. No militant striding, but more of a great, slow, happy meandering down Constitution Avenue, a bit of a hootenany, a lot of picnicking on the park grass. And then there was oratory, some of it fairly inflammatory, but much of it audible to only a fraction of the throng—and, as NAACP [National Association for the Advancement of Colored People] chieftain Roy Wilkins noted, not too important in the proceedings anyway.

Perhaps because it was so vast—it certainly numbered over 100,000, as predicted, and the police estimated it was twice that—the throng that poured into the city from every direction paid scant heed to its supposedly unified command. A good half hour ahead of schedule, it began moving from the Washington Monument toward the Lincoln Memorial, and its "leaders" had to scramble to get up front.

Though it paid so little attention to orders, this great grouping was nevertheless anything but disorderly. Those like Louisiana's Sen. Long who kept referring to it as a "mob" had failed to go take a look at it. The crowd wasn't merely well dressed and well behaved; it was in good and gentle temper. It sang as it moved, and in tones not strident but soft.

Preparing for the Demonstration

By late yesterday not all the delegations had yet boarded their buses, planes, trains or cars to get out of town, so some trouble was still considered possible. But it seemed that Washington had been over-fearful. Many downtown shops had closed; many young white women had decided not to come to work at their offices; some vacationing suburbanites had nervously asked neighbors to guard their homes against violent intrusion. And a fantastic array of police power had been assembled, sufficient to stamp out insurrection. Standing almost elbow to elbow as the marchers passed by, the police and national guardsmen found they had little to do but beam benevolently.

A rumor that a bomb had been planted in the Washington Monument proved to be false, and a minor counter-demonstration by George Lincoln Rockwell's American Nazis fizzled after only one of his deputies was arrested.

As the rally broke up the Red Cross said it had treated 1,800 people, none with serious injuries. Many fell over tent poles and down steps. There were two epilepsy seizures and "one suspected pregnancy," according to the Associated Press.

Compared with the catastrophe facilities that had been set up by the Red Cross, the casualties were relatively light. Fortunately, Washington's often fearsome weather turned out, like the crowd itself, sunny but cool.

Slow Response from Legislators

As all the experts were predicting, this mass "lobbying" for civil rights produced no immediate visible success on Capitol Hill. A good many legislators turned up at the Lincoln Memorial—and before that some even ordered special meetings with constituents proclaimed over the amplifying system at the Monument grounds. "Congressman Stratton will meet with you New Yorkers at the tree behind the platform," it bawled. "Sen. Ribicoff will see Connecticut marchers across the street." But men like these were clearly lined up for civil rights legislation long before.

Senate Majority Leader Mansfield met with march leaders, but he has no intention of letting the Senate tackle civil rights till it gets rid of other matters. In the House, Judiciary Committee Chairman Celler decided he would have to put off further meetings on legislation until the week of Sept. 9, because so many Congressmen are heading home for an unofficial Labor Day vacation.

The Wide Impact of Media Coverage

Still, it is hard to avoid the feeling that the day's events will have some genuine impact upon the nation's course, diffuse though it may be. Unless all the cigaret and hair-spray salesmen are crazy, advertising pays—and there is little question that the civil rights people achieved a tremendous advertising display, at minimum cost. Telstar [communications satellite] even was splashing it to Europe.

If requests for police press passes are any measure, coverage by resident and out-of-town newspapermen and broadcasters approached a stampede. The publicity impact around the country may be partly favorable and partly quite the opposite. But it will presumably have some result, and not just on the drive for Congressional legislation but on local campaigns for jobs, for voting rights, for demands to be served in public places. The thousands who actually participated return to their cities under exhortation to spur action. These include not just Negroes but many earnest white folk—church groups especially—who by their own account are just getting into the movement.

Leadership of this "march" was multiple, and the orators weren't all saying the same things. For example, Autoworker President Walter Reuther was using the platform to "call upon Congress to enact without delay the civil rights program proposed by President Kennedy." But John Lewis, head of the Stu-

Martin Luther King Jr. and A. Philip Randolph led thousands of people to the nation's capital to peacefully demand civil rights.

dent Non-Violent Coordinating Committee was saying, "We cannot support the Administration's civil rights bill, for it is too little and too late."

A Call for Increased Action

At a time when a good many Negro leaders are privately figuring the emphasis should swing away from demonstrations to such other techniques as boycotts, young Mr. Lewis was arguing loudly for more street action. His language, easily the most violent of the day, is perhaps worth noting for the record:

"All of us must get in the revolution. Get in and stay in the streets of every city, every village and every hamlet of this nation, until true freedom comes, until the revolution is complete. In the delta of Mississippi, in Southwest Georgia, in Alabama, Harlem, Chicago, Detroit, Philadelphia and all over this nation. The black masses are on the march.

"We won't stop now. All of the forces of [Mississippi senator James] Eastland, [Mississippi governor Ross] Barnett, [Alabama governor George] Wallace, and [South Carolina senator Strom] Thurmond won't stop this revolution. The time will come when we will not confine our marching to Washington. We will march through the South, through the heart of Dixie, the way Sherman did. We shall pursue our own 'scorched earth' policy and burn Jim Crow to the ground—nonviolently. We shall fragment the South into a thousand pieces and put them back together in the image of democracy. We will make the action of the past few months look petty. And I say to you, wake up America!"

Which is a pretty strong way of putting it—and the crowd wanted to hear some strong talk. Speaker after speaker hammered the idea that change must come rapidly—many said "now."

But it may have some significance that the gathering also gave much applause to Ledger Smith, of Chicago, whose distinction was that he made his trip to Washington entirely on roller skates.

When the crowd was speaking for itself, it spoke in song. Songs were coming out of the buses as they were parked. They rang out of a dozen places on the Monument hillside, in blithe disregard of the official program being presented at the same time. They came from the mass as it moved. The tone was unmistakably gay. And the theme song of this movement has words that do not sound completely impatient: "We shall overcome . . . some day; we shall walk hand in hand . . . some day."

I Have a Dream

By Martin Luther King Jr.

Civil rights leader, Martin Luther King Jr. had waged a campaign against segregation and other racist policies since the mid-1950s. His belief in nonviolent protest garnered great respect, and his victories brought his cause national prominence. By the mid-1960s, however, civil rights demonstrations brought increasingly violent responses from state authorities. In 1963, King organized protests in Birmingham in which police attacked protesters with police dogs and fire hoses. These increasing acts of violence led King to coordinate with civil rights activist A. Philip Randolph in developing a national march on the nation's capital in Washington, D.C., a demonstration that attracted more than 250,000 protesters. This speech, delivered at the Washington protest on August 28, 1963, recognizes that all men are equal and are capable of integration without denying any citizen his or her rights. Unfortunately King's message of nonviolence, a prominent theme throughout this and other speeches, was shunned by younger black activists who listened to leaders advocating equality by any means necessary. King's dedication and persistence were rewarded when President Johnson signed into law, the following summer, the Civil Rights Act of 1964.

I am happy to join with you today in what will go down in history as the greatest demonstration for freedom in the history of our nation.

Fivescore years ago, a great American, in whose symbolic shadow we stand today, signed the Emancipation Proclamation. This momentous decree came as a great beacon light of hope to millions of Negro slaves who had been seared in the flames of withering injustice. It came as a joyous daybreak to end the long night of their captivity.

But one hundred years later, the Negro still is not free. One hundred years later, the life of the Negro is still sadly crippled by the manacles of segregation and the chains of discrimination. One hundred years later, the Negro lives on a lonely island of poverty in the midst of a vast ocean of material prosperity. One hundred years later, the Negro is still languished in the corners of American society and finds himself an exile in his own land. And so we've come here today to dramatize a shameful condition.

Seeking to Fulfill a Promise

In a sense we've come to our nation's capital to cash a check. When the architects of our republic wrote the magnificent words of the Constitution and the Declaration of Independence, they were signing a promissory note to which every American was to fall heir. This note was a promise that all men, yes, black men as well as white men, would be guaranteed the "unalienable Rights of Life, Liberty, and the pursuit of Happiness." It is obvious today that America has defaulted on this promissory note insofar as her citizens of color are concerned. Instead of honoring this sacred obligation, America has given the Negro people a bad check, a check which has come back marked "insufficient funds."

But we refuse to believe that the bank of justice is bankrupt. We refuse to believe that there are insufficient funds in the great vaults of opportunity of this nation. And so we've come to cash this check, a check that will give us upon demand the riches of freedom and the security of justice.

We have also come to this hallowed spot to remind America of the fierce urgency of now. This is no time to engage in the luxury of cooling off or to take the tranquilizing drug of gradualism. Now is the time to make real the promises of democracy. Now is the time to rise from the dark and desolate valley of segregation to the sunlit path of racial justice. Now is the time to lift our nation from the quicksands of racial injustice to the solid rock of brotherhood. Now is the time to make justice a reality for all of God's children.

A Demand for Civil Rights

It would be fatal for the nation to overlook the urgency of the moment. This sweltering summer of the Negro's legitimate discontent will not pass until there is an invigorating autumn of freedom and equality. Nineteen sixty-three is not an end, but a beginning. And those who hope that the Negro needed to blow off steam and will now be content will have a rude awakening if the nation returns to business as usual. There will be neither rest nor tranquillity in America until the Negro is granted his citizenship rights. The whirlwinds of revolt will continue to shake the foundations of our nation until the bright day of justice emerges.

Uphold a Nonviolent Struggle

But there is something that I must say to my people, who stand on the warm threshold which leads into the palace of justice: In the process of gaining our rightful place, we must not be guilty of wrongful deeds. Let us not seek to satisfy our thirst for freedom by drinking from the cup of bitterness and hatred. We must forever conduct our struggle on the high plane of dignity and discipline. We must not allow our creative protest to degenerate into physical violence. Again and again, we must rise to the majestic heights of meeting physical force with soul force. The marvelous new militancy which has engulfed the Negro community must not lead us to a distrust of all white people, for many of our white brothers, as evidenced by their presence here today, have come to realize that their destiny is tied up with our destiny. And they have come to realize that their freedom is inextricably bound to our freedom. We cannot walk alone.

And as we walk, we must make the pledge that we shall always march ahead. We cannot turn back. There are those who are asking the devotees of civil rights, "When will you be satisfied?"

Until Justice Rolls Down

We can never be satisfied as long as the Negro is the victim of the unspeakable horrors of police brutality. We can never be satisfied as long as our bodies, heavy with the fatigue of travel, cannot gain lodging in the motels of the highways and the hotels of the cities. We cannot be satisfied as long as the Negro's basic mobility is from a smaller ghetto to a larger one. We can never be satisfied as long as our children are stripped of their selfhood and robbed of their dignity by signs stating "for whites only." We cannot be satisfied as long as a Negro in Mississippi cannot vote and a Negro in New York believes he has nothing for which to vote. No, no, we are not satisfied and we will not be satisfied until justice rolls down like waters and righteousness like a mighty stream.

I am not unmindful that some of you have come here out of great trials and tribulations. Some of you have come fresh from narrow jail cells. Some of you have come from areas where your quest for freedom left you battered by the storms of persecution and staggered by the winds of police brutality. You have been the veterans of creative suffering. Continue to work with the faith that unearned suffering is redemptive. Go back to Mississippi, go back to Alabama, go back to South Carolina, go back to Georgia, go back to Louisiana, go back to the slums and ghettos of our northern cities, knowing that somehow this situation can and will be changed. Let us not wallow in the valley of despair.

I Have a Dream

I say to you today, my friends, so even though we face the difficulties of today and tomorrow, I still have a dream. It is a dream deeply rooted in the American dream.

I have a dream that one day this nation will rise up and live out the true meaning of its creed: "We hold these truths to be self-evident, that all men are created equal."

I have a dream that one day on the red hills of Georgia, the sons of former slaves and the sons of former slave owners will be able to sit down together at the table of brotherhood.

I have a dream that one day even the state of Mississippi, a state sweltering with the heat of injustice, sweltering with the heat of oppression, will be transformed into an oasis of freedom and justice.

I have a dream that my four little children will one day live in a nation where they will not be judged by the color of their skin but by the content of their character. I have a dream today.

I have a dream that one day down in Alabama, with its vicious racists, with its governor having his lips dripping with the words of "interposition" and "nullification," one day right there in Alabama little black boys and black girls will be able to join hands with little white boys and white girls as sisters and brothers. I have a dream today.

I have a dream that one day every valley shall be exalted, and every hill and mountain shall be made low; the rough places will be made plain, and the crooked places will be made straight; and the glory of the Lord shall be revealed, and all flesh shall see it together.

Creating Change Through Hope

This is our hope. This is the faith that I go back to the South with. With this faith we will be able to hew out of the mountain of despair a stone of hope. With this faith we will be able to transform the jangling discords of our nation into a beautiful symphony of brotherhood. With this faith we will be able to work together, to pray together, to struggle together, to go to jail together, to stand up for freedom together, knowing that we will be free one day. This will be the day, this will be the day when all of God's children will be able to sing with new meaning:

> My country, 'tis of thee, sweet land of liberty, of thee I sing.
> Land where my fathers died, land of the pilgrim's pride,
> From every mountainside, let freedom ring!

And if America is to be a great nation, this must become true.

And so let freedom ring from the prodigious hilltops of New Hampshire.

Let freedom ring from the mighty mountains of New York.

Let freedom ring from the heightening Alleghenies of Pennsylvania.

Let freedom ring from the snowcapped Rockies of Colorado.

Let freedom ring from the curvaceous slopes of California.

But not only that: Let freedom ring from Stone Mountain of Georgia.

Let freedom ring from Lookout Mountain of Tennessee.

Let freedom ring from every hill and molehill of Mississippi.

From every mountainside, let freedom ring.

And when this happens, when we allow freedom [to] ring, when we let it ring from every village and every hamlet, from every state and every city, we will be able to speed up that day when all of God's children, black men and white men, Jews and Gentiles, Protestants and Catholics, will be able to join hands and sing in the words of the old Negro spiritual:

> Free at last! Free at last!
> Thank God Almighty, we are free at last!

The Birmingham Church Bombing

By the *Los Angeles Times*

On a quiet Sunday morning, September 15, 1963, four little black girls—Denise McNair, Carole Robertson, Cynthia Wesley, and Addie Mae Collins—prepared for their Sunday school lessons in the basement of the Birmingham Sixteenth Street Baptist Church. In the same basement was a bomb placed there by segregationists. All four of the girls were killed when the bomb exploded, and twenty-three other people were injured in the blast. When word spread, angry blacks rioted, and the civil authorities responded with great violence. During the rest of the day, two other black youths were killed by police, compounding the desperation.

The bombing was a result of heightened tensions in the city after a federal court ordered its schools to be integrated. Governor George Wallace chose to defy this order and urged his followers to do the same, but in September, Birmingham schools were compelled to integrate. Black leaders and moderate whites alike tried to prepare their communities for the inevitable mixing of the races in an effort to forestall the previous riots that had taken place in the spring of 1963, when police and firemen used dogs and fire hoses on demonstrating blacks. White segregationists, however, considered the forced integration as a call to action.

The following *Los Angeles Times* article from September 16, 1963, examines the events of the bombing and reveals the shocked response of the Birmingham community. The blast, combined with other shameful Alabama events, such as the dogs and fire hoses of 1963, and the

"Birmingham Bomb Kills Four Girls in Negro Church; Two Boys Slain," *Los Angeles Times*, September 16, 1963.

beatings of demonstrators as they began the Selma to Montgomery march in 1964, contributed to the passage of the Civil Rights Act of 1964, the Voting Rights Act of 1965, and the death of segregation in the South. It is also important to note that on September 18, 1963, Martin Luther King Jr. delivered a eulogy for the bombing victims. He stated that the violence surrounding their deaths should not tarnish the civil rights movement. Instead, he encouraged the community to fight against this violence by increasing their nonviolent actions in the effort to achieve equality.

Four Negro girls were blasted to death Sunday and 23 persons injured in the daylight bombing of a church here, setting off more violence.

Within hours after the dynamite explosion shattered an already shaky racial calm, two Negroes were killed in shootings and three other persons were wounded.

Police said two white youths fatally shot a 13-year-old Negro boy shortly after policemen shot to death Johnnie Robinson, a 16-year-old Negro. Officers said the older boy was killed as they fired over his head when they say him throwing rocks at cars.

In another shooting, a white man was wounded by a Negro, police said. Another white man was wounded in a robbery attempt by a Negro.

Rock-throwing by Negroes was reported in many areas of the city.

Pleading Against Retaliation

Leaders of the 125,000 Negroes pleaded against retaliation for the bombing which brought a climax of horror to the city's first week of school desegregation.

Mayor Albert Boutwell, voicing shock and disbelief, urged everyone to keep off the streets. Leaders of a white segregationist group seeking to start private schools called off a rally and asked followers to go home.

The bombing, which fanned racial fires to new heat, came during Sunday school. The lesson was "The love that forgives."

Police and Troops Patrol Streets

Heavy police patrols roved the city as night fell. They sealed off the bomb-shattered Sixteenth Street Baptist Church, used last summer as an assembly point for anti-segregation marches.

Gov. George Wallace rushed in 300 state troopers.

The governor alerted 500 National Guardsmen in Birmingham. Numerous policemen from surrounding towns and counties were called in.

"The entire forces of the state will be utilized to maintain law and order," said Wallace in a statement.

Dr. Martin Luther King Jr., Atlanta Negro minister who led a summer desegregation campaign here, immediately prepared to come to Birmingham "to plead with my people to remain non-violent in the face of this terrible provocation."

Children Tragically Killed

Killed in the dynamite bombing were Cynthia Wesley, Carol Robertson and Addie Mae Collins, all 14, and Denice McNair, 11.

They apparently were in a lounge in the basement of the old brick church. Cynthia Wesley was hit by the full force of the blast.

She could be identified only by clothing and a ring.

Cynthia and Carol were on the youth board of ushers. The other two victims were to have sung in the youth choir.

This was Youth Day at 16th St. Baptist Church.

Police Lt. Maurice House estimated that 10 sticks of dynamite made up the deadly bomb which apparently was planted in a stairway about 4 ft. below ground level outside the building.

Chunks of concrete, twisted metal and shattered glass were hurled with bullet force against nearby buildings. Several cars were wrecked, twisted and ripped. Glass was everywhere.

"It's just making hate," said a Negro bystander, 38-year-old Andrew Anderson, former professional fighter. "This town is gone now . . . I know it's gone."

Public Shock at the Blast

Mayor Boutwell, expressing deep concern over the prospect of "a great deal of unrest," wept after he learned of the church bombing.

"I never could conceive that anyone existed with such universal malice," he said, tears in his eyes. "I fear that the situation will become worse."

When the explosion came, there were approximately 200 persons in the church, said the pastor. About 80 were in basement classrooms.

The Justice Department said FBI agents, on the scene within minutes, would make a full investigation. Sent into Birmingham were Joseph Dolan and John Nolan, two top aides of Atty. Gen. Robert F. Kennedy.

A department spokesman said that Asst. Atty. Gen. Burke Marshall would also fly to Birmingham. Marshall, in charge of the civil rights division, mediated the civil rights crisis in Birmingham last spring.

Crowds of Negroes gathered quickly after the blast.

Some of them wept. Others cursed.

A Negro mother, clasping a shoe in her hands, wept softly on another woman's shoulder.

The resentment welled.

"I wish I could get my hands on the ones that did it," several Negroes said.

The scream of sirens filled the air as ambulance after ambulance pulled up to the scene of destruction.

The police riot squad moved in and a riot tank roamed the area as the angered Negroes gathered. But there was no serious dis-

Civil rights activists march in Washington, D.C., in memory of the four children killed in the Birmingham church bombing.

order around the church. A few rocks were thrown.

Policemen fired several rounds from shotguns and rifles into the air. The Negroes dispersed.

Two white men were questioned briefly after the bombing. They were released a few hours later. . . .

Action Stems from Hate

In Montgomery, Gov. Wallace offered a $5,000 state reward for apprehension of the bombers.

The Rev. King, in Atlanta, issued this statement:

"I am deeply appalled and distressed that such a barbaric and inhuman act can continue to take place in the United States. To-day's bombing was a crime against humanity. Gov. Wallace is largely responsible for these vicious murders, for his irresponsible words and actions have created the atmosphere for violence and murder all over the state of Alabama.

"It must also be said that this tragic harvest of murder is a result of the seeds of apathy and compromise planted all over the nation. Our whole country should enter into a day of prayer and repentance for this terrible crime."

Inside the Blast Scene

State troopers and police were placed on the alert for a 1960 model auto carrying two men reportedly seen near the church before the blast.

The blast scene was a tragic, pathetic sight. Glass littered the street. Numbed parents wandered about wordlessly. Several cars were wrecked. Chunks of concrete hurled with bullet-like force were imbeded in the cars.

The inside of the church was strewn with glass and debris. In the immediate area of the explosion, the walls were crumbled, a staircase was blown loose and boards snapped like matches lay about.

The heaviest impact was in a small room which appeared to be a lounge. The opposite wall, composed of mortar and bricks, was shattered. But the floor above the blast and most of the basement floor were not severely damaged.

Windows were shattered in buildings more than a block away.

Previous Bombings

The church is only one block away from a Negro motel which was bombed after the anti-segregation demonstrations last spring.

King had been living in the motel. No one was hurt. The same night, the parsonage home of King's brother, the Rev. A.D. King, also was bombed with no casualties.

Birmingham has had more than 40 bombings, apparently connected with the racial situation, in recent years. This is the first time anyone has been killed. No one has been convicted in the bombings.

Police Capt. Jack Warren credited work of an unnamed Negro civil defense captain for preventing an outbreak of violence at the church following the explosion.

"I feared for my life," said Warren, one of the first officers on the scene. "I tried to disperse the crowd with my megaphone, but was having no luck. Then the Negro civil defense official came up with his bullhorn.

"He set up ropes and gradually the crowds dispersed."

The Assassination of John F. Kennedy

By Jacqueline Kennedy and Lee Rankin

On November 22, 1963, President John F. Kennedy arrived in Dallas to take part in activities designed to promote his reelection campaign. Planned for later that day were several events including a motorcade through downtown Dallas, a luncheon speech at the Trade Mart Center, and a flight to Austin where the president would attend a reception and speak at a Democratic fund-raising dinner. While participating in the motorcade, the convertible in which the president rode passed in front of the Texas School Book Depository Building. The car contained the president and Mrs. Kennedy as well as Texas governor John B. Connally and his wife. Seconds later shots resounded in rapid succession. It took a few moments for passengers and onlookers to realize that President Kennedy and Governor Connally had been hit by an assassin's bullet. The shooter was later captured and identified as Lee Harvey Oswald.

President Kennedy was taken to Parkland Hospital, where shortly after his arrival, he was pronounced dead. President John F. Kennedy represented the possibilities of a nation. His efforts to achieve a nuclear test ban treaty with the Soviet Union, his commitment to fighting communism, and his dedication to civil rights were vanquished within a few short moments. His wife, Jacqueline Kennedy, riding in the car with her husband served as a witness to the horrific event. Mrs. Kennedy was one of several people to be questioned later by the Warren Commission, a federal panel headed by Supreme Court justice Earl Warren that was given the task of investigating the president's death. Lee Frankin was General Counsel to the Warren Commission. His job was to act as a liai-

Jacqueline Kennedy, testimony before the Warren Commission, Georgetown, CT, 1963.

son between the CIA and FBI investigators. Later, he was also asked to be Special Prosecutor to the Watergate hearings. In the following excerpt from the Warren Commission testimony, Mrs. Kennedy gives the details of the shooting from her perspective as a witness.

The Chairman [Supreme Court chief justice Earl Warren]. The Commission will be in order. Mrs. Kennedy, the Commission would just like to have you say in your own words, in your own way, what happened at the time of the assassination of the President. [General counsel for the Warren Commission] Mr. [Lee] Rankin will ask you a few questions, just from the time you left the airport until the time you started for the hospital. And we want it to be brief. We want it to be in your own words and want you to say anything that you feel is appropriate to that occasion.

Would you be sworn, please, Mrs. Kennedy?

Do you solemnly swear that the testimony you give before the Commission will be the truth, the whole truth, and nothing but the truth, so help you God?

Mrs. Kennedy. I do.

The Chairman. Would you be seated.

Mr. Rankin. State your name for the record.

Mrs. Kennedy. Jacqueline Kennedy.

Mr. Rankin. And you are the widow of the former President Kennedy?

Mrs. Kennedy. That is right.

Mr. Rankin. You live here in Washington?

Mrs. Kennedy. Yes.

Along the Parade Route

Mr. Rankin. Can you go back to the time that you came to Love Field on Nov. 22 and describe what happened there after you landed in the plane?

Mrs. Kennedy. We got off the plane. The then Vice President [Lyndon B. Johnson] and Mrs. Johnson were there. They gave us flowers. And then the car was waiting, but there was a big crowd there, all yelling, with banners and everything. And we went to shake hands with them. It was a very hot day. And you went all along a long line. I tried to stay close to my husband and lots of times you get pushed away, you know, people leaning over and pulling your hand. They were very friendly.

And, finally, I don't know how we got back to the car. I think Congressman [Bill] Thomas somehow was helping me. There was lots of confusion.

Mr. Rankin. Then you did get into the car. And you sat on the left side of the car, did you, and your husband on your right?

Mrs. Kennedy. Yes.

Mr. Rankin. And was Mrs. [Nellie] Connally—

Mrs. Kennedy. In front of me.

Mr. Rankin. And Governor [John] Connally to your right in the jump seat?

Mrs. Kennedy. Yes.

Mr. Rankin. And Mrs. Connally was in the jump seat?

Mrs. Kennedy. Yes.

Mr. Rankin. And then did you start off on the parade route?

Mrs. Kennedy. Yes.

Mr. Rankin. And were there many people along the route that you waved to?

Mrs. Kennedy. Yes. It was rather scattered going in.

Once there was a crowd of people with a sign saying something like "President Kennedy, please get out and shake our hands, our neighbors said you wouldn't."

Mr. Rankin. Did you?

Mrs. Kennedy. And he stopped and got out. That was, you know, like a little suburb and there were not many crowds. But then the crowds got bigger as you went in.

Mr. Rankin. As you got into the main street of Dallas were there very large crowds on all the streets?

Mrs. Kennedy. Yes.

Mr. Rankin. And you waved to them and proceeded down the street with the motorcade?

Mrs. Kennedy. Yes. And in the motorcade, you know, I usually would be waving mostly to the left side and he was waving mostly to the right, which is one reason you are not looking at each other very much. And it was terribly hot. Just blinding all of us.

Mr. Rankin. Now, do you remember as you turned off of the main street onto Houston Street?

Mrs. Kennedy. I don't know the name of the street.

Mr. Rankin. That is that one block before you get to the Depository Building.

Mrs. Kennedy. Well, I remember whenever it was, Mrs. Connally said, "We will soon be there." We could see a tunnel in front of us. Everything was really slow then. And I remember thinking it would be so cool under that tunnel.

Mr. Rankin. And then do you remember as you turned off of Houston onto Elm right by the Depository Building?

Mrs. Kennedy. Well, I don't know the names of the streets, but I suppose right by the Depository is what you are talking about?

Mr. Rankin. Yes; that is the street that sort of curves as you go down under the underpass.

Mrs. Kennedy. Yes; well, that is when she said to President Kennedy, "You certainly can't say that the people of Dallas haven't given you a nice welcome."

Mr. Rankin. What did he say?

Mrs. Kennedy. I think he said—I don't know if I remember it or I have read it, "No, you certainly can't," or something. And you know then the car was very slow and there weren't very many people around.

And then—do you want me to tell you what happened?

Mr. Rankin. Yes; if you would, please.

My Husband Never Made Any Sound

Mrs. Kennedy. You know, there is always noise in a motorcade and there are always motorcycles beside us, a lot of them backfiring. So I was looking to the left. I guess there was a noise, but it didn't seem like any different noise really because there is so much noise, motorcycles and things. But then suddenly Governor Connally was yelling, "Oh, no, no, no."

Mr. Rankin. Did he turn toward you?

Mrs. Kennedy. No; I was looking this way, to the left, and I heard these terrible noises. You know. And my husband never made any sound. So I turned to the right. And all I remember is seeing my husband, he had this sort of quizzical look on his face, and his hand was up, it must have been his left hand. And just as I turned and looked at him, I could see a piece of his skull and I remember it was flesh colored. I remember thinking he just looked as if he had a slight headache. And I just remember seeing that. No blood or anything.

And then he sort of did this [indicating], put his hand to his forehead and fell in my lap.

And then I just remember falling on him and saying, "Oh, no, no, no," I mean, "Oh my God, they have shot my husband." And

"I love you, Jack," I remember I was shouting. And just being down in the car with his head in my lap. And it just seemed an eternity.

You know, then, there were pictures later on of me climbing out the back. But I don't remember that at all.

Mr. Rankin. Do you remember Mr. [special agent Clinton] Hill coming to try to help on the car?

Mrs. Kennedy. I don't remember anything. I was just down like that.

And finally I remember a voice behind me, or something, and then I remember the people in the front seat, or somebody, finally knew something was wrong, and a voice yelling, which must have been Mr. Hill, "Get to the hospital," or maybe it was Mr. [special agent Roy] Kellerman, in the front seat. But someone yelling. I was just down and holding him. . . .

Two or Three Shots?

Mr. Rankin. Do you have any recollection of whether there were one or more shots?

Mrs. Kennedy. Well, there must have been two because the one that made me turn around was Governor Connally yelling. And it used to confuse me because first I remembered there were three and I used to think my husband didn't make any sound when he was shot. And Governor Connally screamed. And then I read the other day that it was the same shot that hit them both. But I used to think if I only had been looking to the right I would have seen the first shot hit him, then I could have pulled him down, and then the second shot would not have hit him. But I heard Governor Connally yelling and that made me turn around, and as I turned to the right my husband was doing this [indicating with hand at neck]. He was receiving a bullet. And those are the only two I remember.

And I read there was a third shot. But I don't know.

Just those two.

Mr. Rankin. Do you have any recollection generally of the speed that you were going, not any precise amount.

Mrs. Kennedy. We were really slowing turning the corner. And there were very few people.

Mr. Rankin. And did you stop at any time after the shots, or proceed about the same way?

Mrs. Kennedy. I don't know, because—I don't think we

stopped. But there was such confusion. And I was down in the car and everyone was yelling to get to the hospital and you could hear them on the radio, and then suddenly I remember a sensation of enormous speed, which must have been when we took off.

Mr. Rankin. And then from there you proceeded as rapidly as possible to the hospital, is that right?

Mrs. Kennedy. Yes.

The Story We Came For

Mr. Rankin. Do you recall anyone saying anything else during the time of the shooting?

Mrs. Kennedy. No; there weren't any words. There was just Governor Connally's. And then I suppose Mrs. Connally was sort of crying and covering her husband. But I don't remember any words.

And there was a big windshield between—you know—I think. Isn't there?

Mr. Rankin. Between the seats.

Mrs. Kennedy. So you know, those poor men in the front, you couldn't hear them.

Mr. Rankin. Can you think of anything more?

The Chairman. No; I think not. I think that is the story and that is what we came for.

We thank you very much, Mrs. Kennedy.

Mr. Rankin. I would just like to ask if you recall Special Agent Kellerman saying anything to you as you came down the street after you turned that corner you referred to.

Mrs. Kennedy. You mean before the shots?

Mr. Rankin. Yes.

Mrs. Kennedy. Well, I don't, because—you know, it is very hard for them to talk. But I do not remember, just as I don't recall climbing out on the back of the car.

Mr. Rankin. Yes. You have told us what you remember about the entire period as far as you can recall, have you?

Mrs. Kennedy. Yes.

The Chairman. Thank you very much, Mrs. Kennedy.

Establishing a New Policy in South Vietnam

By the U.S. Senate Subcommittee on Public Buildings and Grounds

On October 11, 1963, President John F. Kennedy issued National Security Action Memorandum (NSAM) 263 in which he stated his intention to remove U.S. forces from Vietnam by the end of 1965. This decision came from several conversations he had conducted with General Maxwell D. Taylor and Secretary of Defense Robert S. McNamara. On November 2, three weeks after President Kennedy had published NSAM 263 as an official document from the White House, President Ngo Dinh Diem of South Vietnam and his brother Ngo Dinh Nhu were killed during a military coup. The deaths of the Ngo brothers allegedly increased President Kennedy's desire to withdraw from the region to allow the people of Vietnam to establish a government of their choosing. After President Kennedy's assassination on November 22, President Lyndon Johnson signed NSAM 273, which was supposed to be a continuation of the Kennedy administration's policies in Vietnam. NSAM 273, however, committed more resources to the war effort, and committed troop involvement beyond President Kennedy's projected withdrawal time line. The following selection from *The Pentagon Papers*, compiled by the U.S. Senate Subcommittee on Public Buildings and Grounds, examines the directives of NSAM 273 and establishes it as the guiding document behind U.S. policy in South Vietnam.

The U.S. Senate Subcommittee on Public Buildings and Grounds, *The Pentagon Papers: The Defense Department History of the United States Decisionmaking on Vietnam, Volume III*. Boston: Beacon Press, 1975.

NSAM 273 of 26 November 1963 came just four days after the assassination of President Kennedy and less than a month after the assassination of the Ngo brothers and their replacement by the Military Revolutionary Committee (MRC). NSAM 273 was an interim, don't rock-the-boat document. Its central significance was that although the two assassinations had changed many things, U.S. policy proposed to remain substantially the same. In retrospect, it is unmistakably clear, but it was certainly not unmistakably clear at that time, that this was a period of crucial and accelerated change in the situation in South Vietnam. NSAM 273 reflected the general judgment of the situation in Vietnam that had gained official acceptance during the previous period, most recently and notably during the visit of Secretary [Robert S.] McNamara and General [Maxwell D.] Taylor to Vietnam in late September of that year.

An Early Statement of Troop Withdrawal

This generally sanguine appraisal had been the basis for the recommendation in that report to establish a program to train Vietnamese to carry out, by the end of 1965, the essential functions then performed by U.S. military personnel—by which time "it should be possible to withdraw the bulk of U.S. personnel." As an immediate gesture in this direction, the report recommended that "the Defense Department should announce in the very near future, presently prepared plans to withdraw one thousand U.S. military personnel by the end of 1963." The latter recommendation was acted upon the same day (2 October 1963) by making it part of a White House statement of *U.S. Policy on Vietnam.* This White House statement included the following pronouncement.

> Secretary McNamara and General Taylor reported their judgment that the major part of the U.S. military task can be completed by the end of 1965, although there may be a continuing requirement for a limited number of U.S. training personnel. They reported that by the end of this year the U.S. program for training Vietnamese should have progressed to the point where one thousand U.S. personnel assigned to South Vietnam can be withdrawn.

The visit of the Secretary of Defense and the Chairman of the Joint Chiefs to Saigon at the end of September was followed by the report to the President in early October and agreements reached with the President at the White House early in October following the Diem coup, a special meeting on Vietnam was held at CINCPAC [Commander in Chief, Pacific Command] headquarters on 20 November. Although this Honolulu meeting was marked by some concern over the administrative dislocation that had resulted from the coup of three weeks before, the tone remained one of optimism along the lines of the October 2 report to the President. Ambassador [Henry Cabot] Lodge took note of what he called the "political fragility" of the new regime, but he was on the whole optimistic, and even mentioned that the statement on U.S. military withdrawal was having a continued "tonic" effect on the Republic of Vietnam (RVN). General Harkins in his report mentioned a sharp increase in Viet Cong (VC) incidents right after the coup, but added that these had dropped to normal within a week, and that there had, moreover, been compensating events such as additional Montagnards [tribal groups living in the hilly regions of South Vietnam] coming out of the hills to get government protection. All in all there was some uneasiness, perhaps, about unknown effects of the coup, but nothing was said to suggest that any serious departure was contemplated from the generally optimistic official outlook of late September and early October. And so, with reference to the statements of October 2, NSAM 273 repeated:

President Lyndon Johnson, shown greeting American soldiers, increased U.S. military involvement in Vietnam.

The objectives of the United States with respect to the withdrawal of U.S. military personnel remain as stated in the White House statement of October 2, 1963.

Before examining further the background of NSAM 273—especially the appraisals of the Vietnam situation that it reflected—it is well to review some of the main provisions of that policy statement of 26 November 1963.

Provisions in the Revised NSAM 273

NSAM 273 was not comprehensive, as the McNamara-Taylor report of 2 October had been, nor as NSAM 288 was later to be. Mainly it served to indicate continuance by the new President [Lyndon Johnson] of policies already agreed upon, and to demonstrate full support by the United States of the new government of Vietnam (GVN). Both military and economic programs, it was emphasized, should be maintained at levels as high as those in the time of the Diem regime. In addition, there was an unusual Presidential exhortation—reflecting the internal U.S. dispute over policy concerning Diem and Nhu that had made embarrassing headlines in October—that:

> The President expects that all senior officers of the government will move energetically to insure the full unity of support for established U.S. policy in South Vietnam. Both in Washington and in the field, it is essential that the government be unified. It is of particular importance that express or implied criticism of officers of other branches be assiduously avoided in all contacts with the Vietnamese government and with the press.

NSAM 273 was specifically programmatic so far as SVN [South Vietnam] was concerned only in directing priority of effort to the Delta.

> We should concentrate our efforts, and insofar as possible we should persuade the government of South Vietnam to concentrate its effort, on the critical situation in the Mekong Delta. This concentration should include not only military but political, economic, social, educational and informational effort. We should seek to turn the tide not only of battle but of belief, and we should seek to increase not only the controlled hamlets but the productivity of this area, especially where the proceeds can be held for the advantage of anti-Communist forces.

In general, the policies expressed by NSAM 273 were responsive to the older philosophy of our intervention there, which was that the central function of the U.S. effort was to help the South Vietnamese to help themselves because only if they did the major job themselves could that job in reality be done at all. We would assist stabilization of the new regime and head it in that direction.

> It is a major interest of the United States government that the present provisional government of South Vietnam should be assisted in consolidating itself in holding and developing increased public support.

Stressing the Importance of Vietnamese Control

Definition of the central task in South Vietnam as that of winning the hearts and minds of the people and of gaining for the GVN the support of the people had been the central consideration in the late summer and early fall of what to do about Diem and Nhu. The argument concerning the Diem government centered on the concept that the struggle in South Vietnam could not be won without the support of the South Vietnamese people and that under the Diem regime—especially because of the growing power and dominance of Nhu—the essential popular base was beyond reach. In the 2 October report to the President as well as in the discussions later at Honolulu on 20 November this theme was prominent. The U.S. could not win the struggle, only the Vietnamese could do that. For instance, in the report to the President of 2 October, there were these words in the section on "the U.S. military advisory and support effort."

> We may all be proud of the effectiveness of the U.S. military advisory and support. With few exceptions, U.S. military advisors report excellent relations with their Vietnamese counterparts, whom they characterize as proud and willing soldiers. The stiffening and exemplary effect of U.S. behavior and attitudes has had an impact which is not confined to the war effort, but which extends deeply into the whole Vietnamese way of doing things. *The U.S. advisory effort, however, cannot assure ultimate success. This is a Vietnamese war and the country and the war must in the end be run solely by the Vietnamese. It will impair their independence and de-*

*velopment of their initiative if we leave our advisors in place be-
yond the time they are really needed . . .* [emphasis supplied]

Extremes in U.S. Policy

Policy concerning aid to the Vietnamese may be considered to
range between two polar extremes. One extreme would be our
doing almost everything difficult for the Vietnamese, and the
other would consist of limiting our own actions to provision of
no more than material aid and advice while leaving everything
important to be done by the Vietnamese themselves. Choice of a
policy at any point on this continuum reflects a judgment concerning the basic nature of the problem; i.e. to what extent political and to what extent military; to what extent reasonable by
political means and to what extent resolvable by military means
even by outsiders. But in this case the choice of policy also reflected confidence that success was being achieved by the kind
and level of effort that had already been devoted to this venture.
The policy of NSAM 273 was predicated on such confidence. It
constituted by its reference to the 2 October statement an explicit
anticipation, with tentative time phases expressly stated, of the
assumption by the Vietnamese of direct responsibility for doing
all the important things themselves sometime in 1965, the U.S.
thereafter providing only material aid and non-participating advice at the end of that period. That optimism was explicit in the
report to the President of 2 October wherein the conclusion of
the section on "The US Military Advisory and Support Effort"
consisted of this paragraph:

> Acknowledging the progress achieved to date, there still remains
> the question of when the final victory can be obtained. If, by vic-
> tory, we mean the reduction of the insurgency to something little
> more than sporadic banditry in outlying districts, it is the view of
> the vast majority of military commanders consulted that success
> may be achieved in the I, II, and III Corps area by the end of CY
> 1964. Victory in IV Corps will take longer—at least well into
> 1965. *These estimates assume that the political situation does not
> significantly impede the effort.* [emphasis supplied]

CHRONOLOGY

January 14: Alabama governor George Wallace delivers his inaugural speech, declaring "Segregation now! Segregation forever!"

January 15: The Supreme Court begins hearing arguments on the Gideon case; the eventual ruling on this case guaranteed court-appointed legal representation for all defendants in all cases.

February 20: White supremacists burn the Student Nonviolent Coordinating Committee's (SNCC) voter registration headquarters and four black-owned businesses in Greenwood, Mississippi.

February 28: SNCC members Jimmy Travis, Bob Moses, and Randolph Blackwell are shot at while returning from a voter education and registration meeting in Greenwood, Mississippi.

March 21: Alcatraz Federal Penitentiary in San Francisco, notable for housing several famous prisoners such as Al Capone, closes permanently.

March 27: One hundred twenty black activists are attacked by police with dogs and fire hoses in front of the Wesleyan Methodist Church in Birmingham, Alabama, during an attempt to march on the courthouse to protest voter discrimination.

April 2: A grand jury indicts U.S. Steel and six other manufacturers in a price-fixing investigation.

April 3: Activists working for Martin Luther King's Southern Christian Leadership Conference conduct sit-ins at local diners and other public facilities in Birmingham, Alabama.

April 10: The U.S. nuclear submarine *Thresher*, with a crew of 129, sinks in the Atlantic.

April 11: City officials in Birmingham obtain an injunction preventing protest activities and demonstrations in the downtown area.

April 12: Martin Luther King and Ralph D. Abernathy go to jail in Birmingham for marching in defiance of the Birmingham injunction.

May 2: Birmingham police chief Bull Connor arrests and jails 958 children for marching against the injunction banning protest demonstrations.

May 3: Bull Connor orders fire hoses and police dogs turned against civil rights activists—including women and children—beginning a seven-day period of violence against activists in Birmingham.

May 6: Birmingham police arrest a thousand children and adults, bringing the total number of activists arrested during the first week of May to twenty-five hundred.

May 8: Buddhist monks conduct peaceful protests against President Ngo Dinh Diem's oppression of Buddhists in Vietnam; Buddhist leader Thich Quang Duc threatens mass suicide as a protest if the situation does not change.

May 9: Meetings between white and black leaders negotiate an end to most of the remaining laws condoning segregation in Birmingham.

May 10: The first urban riot of the 1960s occurs in Birmingham. Black rioters burn white-owned property in response to the bombing of black businesses and property.

May 12: Professor Timothy Leary of Harvard is fired from his post for continuing his work with the psychedelic drug LSD.

May 15–16: Astronaut Gordon Cooper completes twenty-two orbits of the earth, breaking the previous Soviet record of seventeen.

May 28: NAACP field secretary Medgar Evers confirms an agreement with city officials to end segregation in Jackson, Mississippi, but the offer is later withdrawn.

June 10: Congress enacts the Equal Pay for Women Act.

June 11: President John F. Kennedy delivers his "Moral Crisis" speech on segregation. Governor Wallace blocks the entrance of the University of Alabama in order to prevent two black students—James Hood and Vivian Malone—from enrolling. After Kennedy federalizes the National Guard, effectively removing Wallace's control of state troops, Wallace is removed without incident, and Hood and Malone are allowed to register, becoming the first two black students to attend the university. Thich Quang Duc sets himself on fire in Vietnam to protest the oppression of Buddhists by the Diem regime.

June 12: Medgar Evers is murdered outside of his home in Jackson, Mississippi.

June 16: Soviet cosmonaut Valentina Tereshkova becomes the first woman in space aboard the module *Vostok 6*.

June 26: President Kennedy, on a ten-day European tour, gives his "Ich bin ein Berliner" speech to a crowd gathered at the Berlin Wall.

July 25: A limited nuclear test ban treaty prohibiting testing in the atmosphere, in space, and underwater is tentatively signed by government representatives of the United States, Great Britain, and the Soviet Union at a meeting in Moscow.

August 28: Two hundred fifty thousand people gather in Washington, D.C., for the March on Washington in support of civil rights; Martin Luther King delivers his "I Have a Dream" speech.

September 9: Governor Wallace broadcasts on national news that he will not allow the integration of public schools in Birmingham.

September 10: Twenty African American children are integrated into the Birmingham public school system.

September 13: Governor Wallace announces his candidacy for president.

September 15: The Sixteenth Street Baptist Church in Birmingham is bombed, killing four black Sunday school students: Addie Mae Collins, 14; Denise McNair, 11; Carole Robertson, 14; and Cynthia Wesley, 11.

October 7: President Kennedy officially signs the first Atomic Test Ban Treaty; SNCC workers conduct Freedom Day in an effort to register black voters in Selma, Alabama.

October 13: A performance by the Beatles at the London Palladium is shown on American television; reactions to the performance were so favorable that the media coin the phrase *Beatlemania.*

November 1: A military coup in South Vietnam overthrows and assassinates President Diem and his family.

November 22: President Kennedy is assassinated in Dallas by Lee Harvey Oswald. Vice President Lyndon B. Johnson is sworn into office as the thirty-sixth president of the United States.

November 24: Dallas business owner Jack Ruby kills accused assassin Lee Harvey Oswald in the basement of the Dallas Police Department on national television.

November 24: President Lyndon Johnson signs a security memorandum stating that the U.S. goal in Vietnam is helping the Saigon government to achieve a military victory over the North Vietnamese Communists.

November 25: President Kennedy is buried at Arlington National Cemetery following a mass at St. Matthew's Roman Catholic Cathedral. The leaders of ninety-two nations attend the funeral, among them Charles de Gaulle of France and Prince Philip of Great Britain.

November 29: President Johnson establishes the Warren Commission, headed by Supreme Court chief justice Earl Warren, to investigate the assassination of President Kennedy.

December 8: Frank Sinatra Jr. is kidnapped in Lake Tahoe, Nevada. He is released three days later, unhurt, in Los Angeles after his father pays a $240,000 ransom. Most of the money is recovered when FBI agents arrest three suspects.

FOR FURTHER RESEARCH

General History

Alexander Bloom, ed., *Long Time Gone: Sixties America Then and Now.* New York: Oxford University Press, 2001.

Betty Friedan, *The Feminine Mystique.* New York: W.W. Norton, 1963.

Roger D. Launius and Bertram Ulrich, *NASA and the Exploration of Space.* New York: Stewart, Tabori, and Chang, 1998.

Civil Rights

E. Culpepper Clark, *The Schoolhouse Door: Segregation's Last Stand at the University of Alabama.* New York: Oxford University Press, 1993.

Medgar Evers, "Why I Live in Mississippi," *Ebony*, November 1958.

Martin Luther King Jr., *A Call to Conscience: The Landmark Speeches of Dr. Martin Luther King, Jr.*, ed. Clayborne Carson and Kris Shepard. New York: Intellectual Properties Management, 2001.

Stephen Lesher, *George Wallace: American Populist.* Reading, MA: Addison-Wesley, 1993.

Anthony Lewis, *Gideon's Trumpet.* New York: Random House, 1964.

Malcolm X, *Malcolm X Speaks: Selected Speeches and Statements*, ed. George Breitman. New York: Grove Weidenfeld, 1965.

William A. Nunnelly, *Bull Connor.* Tuscaloosa: University of Alabama Press, 1991.

Lucas A. Powe Jr., *The Warren Court and American Politics.* Cambridge, MA: Harvard University Press, 2000.

Counterculture

Rick Beard and Leslie Cohen Berlowitz, eds., *Greenwich Village: Culture and Counterculture.* New Brunswick, NJ: Rutgers University Press, 1993.

Albert Goldman, *Freakshow: Misadventures in the Counterculture, 1959–1971.* New York: Cooper Square Press, 2001.

David Horowitz, ed., *Counterculture and Revolution.* New York: Random House, 1972.

Jill Jonnes, *Hep-Cats, Narcs, and Pipe Dreams: A History of America's Romance with Illegal Drugs.* New York: Scribner, 1996.

John F. Kennedy Assassination

Benjamin C. Bradlee, *Conversations With Kennedy.* New York: W.W. Norton, 1975.

James P. Duffy, *The Assassination of John F. Kennedy: A Complete Book of Facts.* New York: Thunder's Mouth Press, 1992.

Seymour M. Hersh, *The Dark Side of Camelot.* Boston: Little, Brown, 1997.

Janet M. Knight, ed., *Three Assassinations: The Deaths of John & Robert Kennedy and Martin Luther King.* 2 vols. New York: Facts On File, 1978.

Athan Theoharis, ed., *A Culture of Secrecy: The Government Versus the People's Right to Know.* Lawrence: University Press of Kansas, 1998.

Tom Wicker, "President Kennedy Shot in Dallas," *New York Times*, November 23, 1963.

The Student Movement

Clayborne Carson, *In Struggle: The SNCC and the Black Awakening of the 1960s.* Cambridge, MA: Harvard University Press, 1995.

Dave Dellinger, *More Power than We Know: The People's Movement Toward Democracy.* Garden City, NY: Anchor Press, 1975.

Marc Jason Gilbert, ed., *The Vietnam War on Campus: Other Voices, More Distant Drums.* Westport, CT: Praeger, 2001.

Howard Zinn, *SNCC: The New Abolitionists.* Boston: Beacon Press, 1964.

Websites

The Alabama Department of Archives and History, www.archives. state.al.us. The Alabama Department of Archives and History documents many of the speeches and writings of both segregationists and integrationists whose work is considered influential in the civil rights movement in Alabama.

The Best of Kennedy Assassination Websites, http://mcadams. posc.mu.edu/bestof.htm. The Best of Kennedy Assassination Websites offers a variety of useful links to websites that cover the Kennedy assassination in depth. This site also contains links to sites claiming that the assassination of President Kennedy was the result of a conspiracy.

The Martin Luther King Papers Project, www.stanford.edu/group/ King. The Martin Luther King Papers Project is a collection of Dr. King's most famous writings and speeches. Extensive information about his life, his involvement in civil rights, and his assassination is also available.

The Sixties Project, http://lists.village.virginia.edu/sixties. The Sixties Project offers a collection of several primary documents that were fundamental in the emergence of the student movement and the antiwar movement.

INDEX